UNAPOLOGETIC

A STORY BY
NATALIE FROST

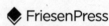 FriesenPress

One Printers Way
Altona, MB R0G 0B0
Canada

www.friesenpress.com

ISBN
978-1-03-913126-2 (Hardcover)
978-1-03-913125-5 (Paperback)
978-1-03-913127-9 (eBook)

1. SELF-HELP, PERSONAL GROWTH, SELF-ESTEEM

Distributed to the trade by The Ingram Book Company

TABLE OF CONTENTS

FORWARD

Welcome, beautiful, thank you for being here with me. I wanted to share something with you before you jump into the book, to give you context. I struggled back and forth on whether or not I wanted to publish my manuscript as myself or under a pseudonym. I want my readers to feel they can trust me and know who I am and what I have gone through, but at the same time . . . I have to protect the people in my story. If I wrote this manuscript under my real name, I would have to change a lot of it so that the individuals in my life are not burdened by what I have written. I believe in people having their privacy, but I also believe in being able to share my story. I truly love everyone who has been in my life—even the ones who have hurt me. I am not a mean person or trying to cause anyone pain. I wrote this to help with my pain and to move forward from it. I do hope that sharing this will help you, the reader, understand that I want to protect people and help others at the same time. Therefore, I thank you for understanding and I hope that at the very least you learn something that can help you and it won't matter who's name is on the front cover!

"You gain strength, courage and confidence by every experience in which you really stop to look fear in the face. You must do the thing you think you cannot do."

—Eleanor Roosevelt

INTRODUCTION

"You can't go back and change the beginning, but you can start where you are and change the ending."

—C.S. Lewis

Once upon a time there was a girl who grew up in the best home, with the best life, no problems, never got in trouble. Ha! I'm just kidding. In this day and age there is no such thing as the perfect life with no issues. I used to believe that there was this fairy tale ending that everyone received as long as they tried in life. I finally realized that "perfect" has a different definition to everyone. No two people's idea of a "perfect life" is the same. My idea of a perfect life was the white picket fences with the beautiful, clean home with two children and my great husband. Along with two dogs and a job that made me happy to get up and go to every day. I dreamed of an amazing group of friends who were always there for each other and made sure spending time together was a top priority. I had planned for all this to happen before the age of thirty. That was my goal. In my eyes, that was a totally doable goal. Thirty seemed so far away at the time. But as the years went by, thirty was catching up quick. And then

BAM, I am thirty-four, with none of those things. Let me back up so you can understand the whole story . . .

I will start with a little background on my childhood to give some perspective. I grew up with parents who met on a blind date and were married at ages nineteen and twenty, shortly after they met. My grandparents were also married young. This is how I grew up, watching these types of relationships and trying to learn from them. There was no screaming, no abuse, no resentment or broken families. We were a big family, who even went on holidays together! Growing up with my cousins was really cool; the bond between us was not something you usually see with cousins. We were all really close in age, so we got along for the most part. We would have sleepovers, fun adventures, day trips and just overall fun memories. So I thought this was what most families were like.

I feel like this false hope of finding my soulmate at a young age made me try to find the perfect life with any guy that I was with. I have always fallen fast and hard with any guy who looked at me or gave me any attention. I told myself, *This could be it, this could be the guy who can give me the "perfect life."* Little did I know that it wasn't the perfect life I was supposed to be searching for with someone—I was supposed to get to know a person to see if I WANTED to spend the rest of my life with him. It shouldn't matter what he can offer in terms of material things. You should actually want to be around the person through thick and thin . . . not just make it work.

I unfortunately missed the memo on that, and I tried to make any guy I dated fit into that cookie cutter form. I would say to myself, *This is the perfect life I want, so now I am going to make him fit into that perfect life whether I believe I deserve better or not.* I never wanted to admit I was settling, or that I was unhappy. I didn't want other people to be right, or for other people to have the life I wanted and I didn't at least try.

I do, still to this day, have to constantly remind myself that back when my parents were young—in the pre-Internet days—it was a lot easier to grow a relationship without temptations to cheat or have readily access to drugs, porn, or other equally bad options for bad decisions.

Nowadays, for kids, in the "online is life" era, they have to compete with social media; the likes and follows are an addiction. The feeling of waking up and quickly grabbing your phone to see if someone sent you a message, liked your post, or to scroll to see what other people are doing with their lives—that is an addiction, and most people do not see that they have a problem.

Think about it for a moment . . . Have you ever left home without your phone on purpose? And if you do happen to forget it, you would turn around and go back for it, wouldn't you? Some people actually have massive anxiety attacks if they cannot find their phone. People can barely go out to eat together without having their phones out, or checking them constantly. I even find myself doing this, which is terrible! I hate seeing people on their phones all the time. But it is honestly an addiction that is hard to break for any age.

On top of the screen time issue, the amount of bullying that is going on in young children in schools is drastically higher due to cyber bullying and the ease of doing it without consequences. The world is so scary now with bombers, drugs in the form of children's candy, chemicals and illnesses that have super bugs. It's no wonder people are looking for someone to care online. It's easy access; you don't even have to get off the couch to get the attention, and you certainly don't have to change your clothes or dress up. You could be sitting in your ratty PJs with a bowl of popcorn and a bottle of wine—they don't know!

Growing up, I was one of those kids who loved to use their imagination, whether it was coming up with games, plays, adventures, or just exploring outside, I loved it! Nowadays—currently the year 2021—we can't even get kids to go outside without an electronic attached to their body. Sometimes I feel like it was better to live in the 1900s, where we were never inside in the summertime. We could hang out with our friends without having someone watching over us. But then I think back to the experiences in my life that could have been avoided if I'd had an outlet, a way to talk to people, or way to look things up. I probably wouldn't have gone through everything I did, at least not alone. I grew up learning to bottle everything that was bugging me, hurting me, scaring me. It was difficult navigating feelings that I didn't quite understand.

All my life I wanted to do something great. I wanted to be known for achieving something that no one else had. I wanted to make a difference in this world. I didn't have a certain path to take; I had no idea where to even start with this dream. I have always said I wanted this, but I don't believe I ever even tried to figure out what that looked like. No, in fact, I have never sat down and said, "Okay, what are we going to do, in order to be great?" Success does not happen overnight, and I think I always knew that; I just wasn't ready to put everything into something I didn't even know would go anywhere. I let myself down in so many ways, and this has been one of my biggest regrets.

My intention in writing this book is to share what I have gone through and how I have risen above it. I am going to share my life story and some of the scary, terrible things I went through alone and the lessons I learned. I am going to be sharing some very personal, upsetting information. Most of it I've never told anyone. I have been ashamed, embarrassed, scared, and I pushed most of it down or tried to forget it. Which has unfortunately caused me a lot of pain in life and now I have to work on healing the past 34 years rather than dealing and healing from the hard times when they come. This is a trait I know that a lot of women do because we don't feel we deserve things, but this is incorrect. Everyone deserves good things in life and everyone deserves to have their dreams come true but we also realize that we have to fight that much harder to get them.

Recently I have been thinking a lot about how much I enjoy writing and I've been trying to find a topic that I believe in, or think would be helpful for someone. I grew up dreaming of how to make a difference in this world and up until now, I could not think of anything. Some recent events have made me realize that telling my story could help someone. I am hoping that by sharing my story and sharing how I might have done things differently, I might just help at least one person. I can honestly say I wish I had listened to people more, and not made some of the choices that I did. I wish I could redo parts of my childhood. I don't regret all of it, but some of the things I did made life a lot harder than it had to be.

I look at kids in 2020 and see them in the Olympics, or traveling the whole world in a year, or becoming amazing CEOs of companies. The drive for kids is really a hit or miss. Some kids will become something great, and others will just get through life coasting. I just wish I would have spent more time doing something great rather than hating myself. I never did the work to make myself better. I never did the work to accept what had happened in my life and move on from it. Each relationship and all the issues that it had was brought into my next one. I thought pushing everything down and "moving on" would work, but I really wasn't moving on.

In the beginning of 2020, I thought about everything I wanted to do in my life that I felt I had missed out on. COVID-19 hit during this time and it felt like a crazy dream. I had never witnessed anything like it before. To put it in perspective, I was an almost thirty-three-year-old woman living with her partner of three years and his two kids. One of them was with us 50/50 and the other one was with us full time, as her mom had not been in the picture since she was about five or six, and she is a teenager now. I had a full time job that allowed me to work from home, which COVID did not affect. HOWEVER—because of COVID, my partner and his kids were home full time. So I had to work with everyone home, and I did not have an office at this time, I would just find space to sit and try and concentrate. I was so stressed, and I dealt with it by drinking a half to one bottle of wine each night. It just took away my grumpy mood, and made me feel free. I felt free, but I gained weight and had zero energy and felt sick ALL of the time. We also got a puppy right before COVID so I was dealing with a new puppy that everyone said they would help me with. (You can't see me, but there was a huge eye roll that went with that statement.) I was miserable trying to deal with everything while no one helped.

So I pushed myself to write things out, pushed through the tough pain and kept drinking. Sometimes while I was writing I ended up going down a dark hole, thinking of all the things I had gone through, getting into the details—but as a weird twist, it actually helped me heal some of the pain that was still hiding. I cried a lot writing this book... but they were healing tears in the end.

I am currently not married, with no kids of my own. I do not own a house (because have you seen the cost of houses and the hoops new home owners have to go through? Yikes). I absolutely do not have a white picket fence or my dream job. I do have a job I enjoy and have been in the industry for over sixteen years. I am working on my self and healing every day. I do not believe giving up is an option because someone needs me. Someone needs to hear my story. And I believe I can one day still have the life I was meant for! Belief is half the battle.

I really just want people to read this and say "if she can do it, why not me?" No matter what pain you've felt, YOU are strong enough to get through it and rise above it, but it all starts with you. You have to believe you can, and fight for what you believe in. Keep going, beautiful, do not give up.

So let's dive right in and see if any of this resonates with you!

"Owning your story is the bravest thing you will ever do."

—Brene Brown

CHAPTER 1

THE NITTY GRITTY

✳ Trigger Warning: Topic of Abuse ✳

"You need to do hard things to be happy in life. Because the hard things ultimately build you up and change your life.
They make the difference between existing and living, between knowing the path and walking it, between a lifetime of empty promises and one filled with progress."

—Marc and Angel

This chapter is not for the faint of heart. Some things in here are going to be unsettling to hear. But I think it is important that we talk about it. Because I didn't, and boy has it affected me in ways I didn't think it could.

I thought growing up meant growing out of the past, but it can follow you if you let it. It will show up when you least want it to, you have given it this power over you. It pulls you down into the dirt and gets all into the nitty gritty of your life. It is not fun, but it is something that people joke about or are too scared to talk about. I know—I was one of those people. I have also included a couple things to note about the different kinds of abuse. There are still some people who believe that there is only one type of abuse and that it can only come from males. This is not true at all. It is not just physical; there is emotional and mental abuse as well. Emotional abuse is the most common form of abuse and yet the least talked about. The below information is from a website called Ananias Foundation and it gives a great breakdown of the definitions of abuse.

What is abuse, anyway?

Abuse, simply stated, is the mistreatment of something that results in harm.

Domestic abuse is when one person mistreats another who is part of their household, family, or is in a dating or marriage relationship with them. While the domestic abuse definition can include mistreatment of an older family member (elder abuse) or a child (child abuse), the kind we are focusing on is hurting our intimate (dating or marriage) partners.

Mistreatment (abuse) comes in different forms. It could be bodily injury or the threat of injury (physical abuse) or words or actions that damage a person's sense of well-being and independence (emotional abuse).

Physical abuse and domestic violence are two terms for the same thing: physical force that hurts someone in our household, family, or in a relationship with us. Here's what is considered domestic violence:

- Pushing or shoving
- Grabbing to restrict movement (stopping a partner from leaving, for example)
- Slapping
- Kicking
- Biting
- Hitting with a fist or object
- Beating up (striking more than once)
- Using a knife or gun

There's a progression of violence from top to bottom, but an answer of 'yes' to any of these is considered domestic violence and battery. Threatening any of these, even if they are not carried out, is considered domestic violence and assault. (Ananias Foundation, n.d.)

Can abuse occur if no one is touched? Yes. Examples of emotional abuse are:

- Controlling your partner's time, space, money, thoughts, or choices such as what they wear
- Monitoring where your partner goes or what they spend money on
- Isolating your partner by not letting them see or talk to others
- Making all of the decisions without your partner's input or consideration of their needs
- Accusing your partner of flirting, having an affair, or being unfaithful when there is little or no evidence they have done so. Read more about jealousy here.
- Getting angry or resentful when your partner is successful in a job or hobby
- Intimidating your partner by making them afraid, including breaking things, punching walls, slamming doors, or throwing objects
- Threatening to hurt your partner, their children, their pets, or damage their property, even if you don't follow through on the threat
- Threatening to hurt yourself, especially when things are not going your way
- Threatening to leave or divorce your partner
- Demeaning your partner with frequent put-downs, name calling, blame, or humiliation
- Saying things that are designed to make your partner feel "crazy" or "stupid"
- Always being right, never apologizing

- Punishing your partner by refusing to talk to them or by withholding affection
- Withholding essential resources like food or money (also called economic abuse)
- Frequent mood swings, where one moment you are loving and affectionate, and the next moment you're angry and threatening
- Frequently and quickly escalating into rage, where you just snap and lose it
- Blaming others for your behavior, especially your parents, partner, or children
- Blaming alcohol, drugs, stress, or other life events for your behavior
- Using sex, money, privileges, or other favors as a way to "make up" after conflict in order to stop feeling guilty
- Acting like your behavior is no big deal, denying the behavior, or telling your partner it's their fault
- Using religious beliefs to justify holding a dominant, authoritarian position over your partner (also called spiritual abuse)
- Attempting to force your partner to keep quiet about your behavior or drop criminal charges

You may be thinking, "So if I'm upset and don't talk to my spouse for an afternoon, or I slip up and call him or her a name in the heat of an argument, that's abuse?" While neither of these actions are ever good, they are not necessarily abuse. In reality, we all do some of these things sometimes. They become abusive when they are repeated frequently.

What if, in reading these lists, you have that awful, gut-wrenching feeling that you fit the definition? Then what? It doesn't have to be that way for you forever. Change is possible. To borrow a quote from Beverly Engel in *The Emotionally Abusive Relationship*: "There are no monsters here, only injured but brave individuals who are seeking to heal themselves from the bondage of their actions." (Ananias Foundation, n.d.)

Now that we have a clearer understanding of abuse—let's jump in.

The Ones Closest to You

The earliest memory I have of some sort of abuse, was when I was younger; I am not even sure what age I was, but old enough to remember. My parents had family friends that had a son around the same time I was born, so we basically grew up together, like cousins but not blood related. We would go on camping trips and visits with the family. It was always a good time. As we got older, he grew into his body. I don't really remember when it started to happen, but he would always ask me, when we were alone, if he could practice kissing with me. At first I liked the attention and didn't really think anything bad about it. I felt like someone noticed me; I wasn't in the shadow of my sister. I had always felt that my sister outshined me in every way. And for once I was the center of someone's attention.

As a kid growing I was told that doctors were the only other people who should be looking at me without clothes on or touching me where it was private. One of the things adults like to ask kids is what do you want to be when you grow up. Doctor was something that would came up. But then I was asked if I would play doctor with my "cousin", it didn't seem like the same kind of doctor I would want to be. As a kid it was exciting to pretend, you know, put on a white jacket, use the plastic doctor tools from Toys "R" Us and try to figure out what is "wrong" with the other person—or just do a check-up. I didn't think anything of it because it was someone I knew and trusted. I felt like I had to do what he said, or he would get upset or make me feel like I was in the wrong. I didn't want to be that person who would feel bad, so I accepted it. Honestly it is a bit of a blur for me, as I apparently tried to block it out, or maybe I was just too young to understand. Only now it has come to light as something I should have told someone about—because of a situation I am in now. I will get to that later on.

As a kid I was told, "Don't let anyone touch you that you don't know or feel comfortable with." That is pretty clear. Stranger = no touching. But what about those you do know and trust . . . then what? For the most part it seems to be the people we trust who actually abuse us because we allow them in, because we are told they are family and we can trust them. In society, it used to feel like you could not say anything that you had to keep things secret, otherwise you were worthless or wrong. In this generation it seems that many people have abuse in their past they never acknowledged. When things are not allowed to see the light of day, you can't heal or move past it. You just push it down and hope it never resurfaces.

In the 2012 Canadian Community Health Survey - Mental Health, 32% of Canadian adults reported that they had experienced some form of abuse before the age of sixteen:

26% had experienced physical abuse;
10% had experienced sexual abuse;
8% had experienced exposure to intimate partner violence
(Government of Canada. 2018)

According to 2016 police report data, among children and youth victims of violence reported to police, 30% were victims of family violence perpetrated by parents, siblings, extended family member or spouse. Girls were four to five times more likely than boys to be victims of child sexual abuse by a family member. Girls between the ages of fourteen to seventeen were almost twice as likely to be victims of family-related violence, compared to their male counterparts. *(Government of Canada. 2018)*

According to data from child welfare agencies in Canada in 2008, children were exposed to the following types of abuse:

– *Exposure to intimate partner violence (34%)*
– *Neglect (34%)*
– *Physical abuse (20%)*

- *Emotional abuse (9%)*
- *Sexual abuse (3%)* (*Government of Canada. 2018*)

Those numbers are quite high and pretty upsetting. So many people have been hurt and then they have to try to live life with that hurt. Some people take it out on their families because that is what was taught to them while growing up and a few will rise above it and not go down the same path. These numbers need to go down, and quickly.

My Own Experience

One time that I remember quite clearly when I was age 8-9, we were going camping somewhere that was a bit of a drive. The family friends I mentioned before came with us. They had a camper trailer and the kids got to sit in the back as we drove. We felt so special to get to do this! It was my sister, his sister, myself and him in the trailer.

He and I were in the trailer lying on the bed, while the other two were doing something up front. We were just talking, and then all of a sudden he climbed on top of me and started to kiss me. This had never happened before and instantly a couple of big emotions came out. I was worried something was going to happen that I didn't want, and he was bigger and stronger than me. He had never climbed on top of me before. A couple other times when he had kissed me we had been sitting or standing.

At this point I pretended it was okay; he wouldn't hurt me. I also didn't have much choice in the matter, as he was stronger than me. He told me to trust him, and I felt like I had to. I felt pretty helpless, but at the same time I was like, *Okay, he must care about me.* In my head, I tried to think this was what caring actually meant.

He held my hands down and kept kissing me. He then moved to pushing himself up against me. At this point, I had no clue what to do. You think it is never going to happen to you, that no one will force themselves on you, and if they did, you would say no! But just by saying no, doesn't mean they will stop.

Lying in the bed, I was numb to everything. I couldn't talk. I couldn't move. All I could think was, *when are we going to get there so I can get away from this?* The hardest part was realizing I would be spending this whole trip trying to avoid him and feeling so stupid for freezing. I was powerless. I tried to convince myself that this was okay, that this was what people did when they cared about each other.

Luckily, the trailer slowed; we had arrived. Needless to say, I kept my distance the rest of the trip and made sure I wasn't alone with him.

You are probably wondering how I made it stop or if it went further . . . to be honest, I think it was the timing that stopped it. I didn't see him for a really long time after that, as we moved away and our parents grew apart. His parents ended up getting a divorce, and my parents didn't really make plans with them after that.

I moved forward and pushed those memories down into a box and locked it away. I never told anyone about this happening as I felt ashamed and just wanted to forget the whole thing.

Reflection

Reflecting back, I am actually shocked I did this. I didn't say no, I didn't fight—I froze. I didn't tell anyone about it. I suffered in silence. But saying that, this was back when I really wanted attention. I always felt like my sister was the golden child. I never felt like I had the closeness with my family that my sister did. I felt like she was always one up on me. That does not excuse it, but I believe this is where I decided attention was only going to come to me if I did what they wanted, or changed myself to be more of what they wanted. Feeling unimportant as a kid made me only date guys who would need me and tell me how important I am to them. Deep down I knew if I dated someone put together, I might not be important to them or needed...I always thought I dated un-put together guys because I wanted to help them and I thought it was about them but now I realize all this time it was about me needing to feel important to someone. I have no idea if this was even how people in my life felt, thinking I was unimportant but that was how I felt and I could never ask them if it was true or not.

Oh Those Bad Boys...

Ever hear people say that nice guys finish last and most girls go after the bad boys? Well if you can't admit that you've been in that situation at some point in your life, then there are bigger problems here. It happens all of the time! So many females are drawn to assholes. It is in ourselves, as we think in our minds bad boys will take care of us. If we need a protector, they will be there; a nice guy, he might not know what the hell to do in a fight. It is something in our brain that finds a bad boy more attractive than not. They have no fear.

When I was in elementary school in grades 5-6, I was in the center of a children's love triangle between the nice guy and the bad boy. *Plot twist*—they were best friends and both knew they were fighting for my attention. I would pass notes between the boys in class; we would have nightly phone calls, and then at school we would all hang out as a group, but I usually stuck with the girls. I liked both of them but I was drawn more to the bad boy; he was mysterious, and I really wanted him to like me. He was the kind of guy who would say something that was borderline mean, then apologize to look like the hero. Clearly he enjoyed making me feel bad so that I would keep chasing him fo the attention. And I did. If he wasn't home when I called, or if he w busy, it would make me want to keep trying to call or to find out w was more important than me. Sound familiar?

Side note, ladies—in case you didn't get the memo, bad ONLY like the chase; they don't like the needy girl. If he's middle of the triangle, he just wants to win over the other g are kind of just playing a part to complete the win. They will treat you very well. I know this probably won't convince yo *bad boys* but it's worth a shot. Also, not all boys who lo boys are actually bad. Sometimes you need to actually get to know them rather than going off of looks. Looks fade, personalities do not.

I don't remember ever fully picking one guy or not. But it went on for a few years, and once we got into middle school the bad boy decided to see how far he could get with me. He asked me to meet him at the park that was in between where we both lived. Boy was I excited and nervous. I had no idea what to expect. I was in for a real surprise . . .

I got up the courage to meet him and I snuck out of the house to go to the park, this was the one and only time I snuck out. I was really excited that he wanted to see me and it was the first time one on one with no one else around. He showed up on his bike as I was waiting on the swings.

Side note: there were no cell phones then; we had to call the house and ask to speak to the person. So to plan to meet at a park at night with no cell phone to confirm where the person was or in the case of an emergency seems crazy now!

After a few moments of the initial excitement I noticed he seemed ? in an asshole mood, as he didn't say too much and he looked off about something. He started to kiss me and put his hand ?irt. I was starting to feel uncomfortable as he was going and fast, massaging my breasts. I told him to slow down, ?d to pinch my nipple really hard. I smacked him on ? I was going home. He said he didn't care, he would I was so hurt by the rejection I stopped and said, him and he had a smirk on his face, like, *Oh, I d my finger.* I just ignored the look and kissed ? him to find someone else. I wanted to be

?f my head and pushed me down to ?y knees but he pressed harder and ? what he wanted me to do and I ? I was doing or what to expect.

10

I said I didn't want to, which he took to mean, *Oh, it's happening.* He unzipped his pants and made me take his penis out. He then pushed my head down so I would go down on him. He held my head so tight that I couldn't move it, and pushed it so deep that I gagged and started coughing but he wouldn't stop, I had tears running down my face. Finally I couldn't do it anymore; I had to use my teeth to make him let go.

I was scared and so unsure of what had just happened. I got up and ran away without a word. I walked home in tears. I remember this night so vividly that I get triggered when someone wants me to perform this act. It would make me freeze; I'd be scared that they would force my head and that I wouldn't be able to move. When I did perform this act, I would cry, I couldn't help it. It has affected me for probably twenty years now.

After that night I can't recall what happened with him. I don't remember if I went back to apologize because I thought it was my fault, or if I just tried to get over him. I do remember that he was not the nicest to me, anytime I saw him. I never really got over the forcefulness he put upon me at such a young age. I knew I wasn't ready for all of that and he took away my power to decide when I was. I believe that sometimes we say things to make it seem like we are ready but when it comes down to it, we aren't. Then we are called a tease and the guilt sets in . . .

Powerless

I think at such a young age, as females, we seem to lose our power and notice that men are at the top. Women have to fight for everything, including the right to make our own body choices. I have never understood how people can take this choice away from people OR make them feel bad for not being ready. How do you know when you are ready, you might be asking? Well, I don't think anyone ever really knows. Society makes us think we have to do something just because everyone else is.

Here is an example. People think they need to lose their virginity before graduating, as if being a virgin makes you a loser or something. If anything, I think the people who do wait for the right people to have sex with, rather than just one night stands or whoever is in front of you at the time, are better off in the long run and probably don't have the trauma that comes from doing things when you aren't ready! They focus on schooling, which then gets you a great job. It makes you independent, not clinging to someone and getting permission from that person to do anything.

After going into middle school, I realized I was no longer the girl that anyone wanted to chase after; I was old news. All of the "popular" boys liked the pretty, popular girls. I ended up finding a good group of people who I did not go to elementary school with. With that, we found a group of guys who always hung out in a small group like us. They were all very nice boys and fun to hang out with. I decided I needed a nice boyfriend. In middle school, a boyfriend meant someone you walked to class with, sometimes exchanged notes and talked on the phone with at night. I am sure this was different for other people, but our group was not interested in drugs, alcohol or "hooking up." It was refreshing to realize you could be yourself and not feel pressured to do things you were not ready for.

The group of us all "dated" each other, and back then it wasn't weird at all. But as you get older that changes, and you get mad when your friend dates your ex. In grade 8, I ended up in another triangle situation, and once again, they were friends.

** This is highly not recommended!! **

I had started dating this guy who was living with his friend and his mom because of some situations at home. So I would go hang out with them together. They both wanted to date me, which made me feel really good, and what was better was that I didn't have to pick one—they were both in my life. The only problem with this situation was that these boys were looking for more than just hand holding. Their group of friends all talked about what they were doing with girls and it makes guys jealous, it seems. I ended up dating one of them but still being able to hang out with the other guy I had a crush on.

I struggled with how to know when the right time was, and if I would know. But I didn't really get a chance to decide, as my boyfriend at the time convinced me to have sex with him. Once that happened . . . that changed everything. Once he felt he had the power over me, which was exactly what he did, he showed me he had power over me. He told me the most awful things to make sure I did not think I could go find someone better. I remember one night he was picking a fight, yelling at me and standing over me. He told me that no one would ever want to be with me, I was worthless. Told me I was lucky that he even wanted me. He would tell me that I was fat, that certain ways I look make me look ugly. When he felt that his yelling wasn't getting through to me, he would push me. Hit my head against the wall, throw me across the room. It got so bad, that I felt like all I could do was go to school, go to his house and then go home, otherwise a fight would happen. I didn't get to hang out with my friends anymore; he isolated me. I was trapped.

I forgot to mention that I was also the one with a license and a car, plus I got a part-time job so I could afford to pay for us to do things. He sat at home and played video games. I supported him at sixteen years old. I did everything for him, and yet I was still told I was worthless. Did you know it takes between three to seven times of hearing something to believe it? That isn't that many times, if you think about it.

The night I remember the most, was when I decided to leave. I was crying so hard, I was hurting. I told him I was leaving, and he chased me down the stairs, yelling at me. I went outside and he continued to yell at me. During this time, I had no idea that the neighbour boys, who were a couple years older, would come outside when they heard us fighting, with chairs and sit and watch. They watched us fighting. They didn't step in, they didn't ask if everything was okay. They just laughed. Later in life I ended up befriending those boys, and they told me that they'd heard us fighting all the time. At the time, this whole event was happening in the driveway. I was hurting and so beyond consolable, and when they told me what they did that night, it actually hurt and brought up a lot of issues for me. I don't understand why they didn't step in. I also had no idea anyone was there watching us. But of course, I just pushed it down further and further. *Push it down, and you'll forget about it, right?*

Another time I remember that was probably the eye opener that I was alone in this whole fucked up situation was the night before I was leaving on vacation with my family. My boyfriend wasn't happy I was going. He decided he wanted to "mark" me so that everyone knew I had a boyfriend. He didn't tell me this was his plan until after we played the game. I will never forget the feeling of this . . . he wanted to play shot for shot. For those of you that don't know what this "game" is, basically each person gets a chance to punch the other person in the arm as hard as they can. Then the next person goes and it goes back and forth until someone gives up. He said it would be fun. Called me mean names when I said I didn't want to. I gave in. He told me to punch him, then he punched me, and then once it hurt too much he would move to another part of my arm. Once I could no longer punch him because my arms hurt so much—while he was obviously fine—he said because I quit he was entitled to giving me snake bites. He grabbed my arm, pushing on one of the bruises that was starting to form. I fell to my knees, and he put his hands on my forearm and quickly swished his hands back and forth until it burned, and I ripped my arm away. I went home in so much pain I could barely keep my arms up to drive. I cried the whole way. I had to rethink my packing now. I had to find clothes that would cover these bruises so my parents wouldn't know. Try and hide your body on a vacation where it is hot and you are going swimming . . .

I let multiple people take away my light. Crush my soul. At the key time of my life where I was growing into my own person and finding my way, I was hiding behind negative self-talk, abuse, and feeling the absolute worst about myself. My biggest regret about my high school experience was having a boyfriend who controlled me. I missed out on so much and because of him, I felt like I had to do what he told me. If he told me to skip class, I would do it. He told me to be late to go home, I would. I was weak. But in my mind, I was being a loyal girlfriend, we were going to get married one day. I actually thought in my head that we were going to get married and I would be happy.

Before we broke up, I found out he was seeing another girl who lived an hour away, for a few months at the end of our relationship. When I found this out and confronted him, he told me he still wanted me in this life, but he had someone who was better than me. He would still tell me to come over and watch him play video games. And of course I jumped up and went to his house to make him take me back. How sad is that? My first real relationship was clearly fucked. I ignored all signs of it because he told me every day that no one would want me, that I couldn't do better than him, so I should just accept it.

Whoever is reading this: **PLEASE DO NOT LISTEN TO THAT!!** Do not listen to them tell you that you don't deserve anything better. I personally guarantee you, if they are saying it, then you do deserve better. Because anyone who says that to you knows that they control you and you actually could do better but they can't. At the time, I thought he was right because he filled my head with pure garbage. Please do not accept that this is true for you. Anyone who actually deserves you would never say this; they would make sure you knew that you deserve the world—not to have your head smashed against a wall, or thrown down the stairs.

Out of Love or Fear?

I have learned that you need to realize whether you are doing something for love or for fear. If you are doing what someone asks of you because you are scared to say no, rather than it filling up your cup with your decision or being strong enough to voice your opinion, then you need to know that you are doing these things out of fear. Obviously some things in life we have to do even when we don't want to, like make our kids food, or pick them up from school. Sometimes we have to do things for people we love, but that is not out of fear, it is out of love for these people. If someone asks you to help them move, and you REALLY don't want to and helping people in a time of need does not fill up your cup or make you happy, then do not say yes.

I know a lot of times we want to just push down all of the pain and move forward. But here is the thing, you cannot move completely forward from the pain if you do not deal with it. Acknowledge it. Understand why you feel the way you do. Talk it out with a friend or a therapist or write it down if that is better. Forgive. Then you can move on. If you do not do these things, and you just bottle it up, or push it down like I did . . . then it will come back in life and bite ya on the ass. It can ruin really great relationships because you are so paranoid about your boyfriend cheating on you or leaving you for someone else. This literally happened in every single relationship that I had. I am not bragging about being cheated on . . . trust me, it is not a nice feeling. But it put me in a spot to constantly be worried about what things meant, or if I should look in his phone. It makes you paranoid. And you know who likes paranoid people? *NO ONE.*

Good Luck Chuck

There is a movie called *Good Luck Chuck*. It is about a guy who sleeps with women and they don't work out for whatever reason and the next guy the girl dates is the one that they marry. This has been my whole dating life. Pretty much every guy I have dated for longer than three months has married the girl they either cheated on me with or broke up with me for. I was with a guy for four years and he went to work up north in Alberta for months on end. He ended up deciding to stay there, and when I had money I flew there to see him. Mind you, looking back, he was working on the oil rigs and making a ton of money and I was the one paying for the ticket to go. Needless to say, the money ended up going to some of his vices, causing him to go broke really quick. After I went to visit the one time, he broke up with me and said the distance wasn't working. I later found out that he had actually been seeing a girl that lived there for six months while we were still together. After we broke up they bought a house together and got engaged.

I am not saying that our relationship was great and that I want him back—hell no. BUT I poured my heart and soul into that relationship. He was supposed to go there to get money so that we could have a good life . . . instead he found someone "better." I do not have the best track record for men I have chosen to care about . . .

Realization

Going through writing this book and really digging deep inside of myself and seeing where this is going to go, I have done a ton of self-reflection and self-forgiveness. One thing I learned is that I never set standards for myself on what I will and will not tolerate in a relationship. I never had that list of deal breakers, times I would say, "Sorry, I won't date you." I had a hypothetical list in my head, but if I liked the guy, I would say to myself, *Aw, it could be worse, I will let this one slide.* Never has one of the items on my list been a reason I wouldn't date a guy. I always said no smokers. Well, I have dated at least three guys who have smoked. Someone who has kids is a no go. Well, I am currently in a relationship with someone who has had previous relationships with women resulting in kids—and not just one mom, but two different moms. Whether they had money, a job, a vehicle, a drinker, a lazy person, anger issues etc., I have dated them all.

I have set myself up to think that it is okay to not have standards and that everyone deserves a chance. I also think that deep down, I felt like, what if I dated someone out of my league, where I was the one who felt like I didn't deserve this person, or intimidated by their awesomeness. What if I felt like I wasn't the one good enough in the relationship? I guess in my mind, a relationship was supposed to have someone who needed help, so the other had to fix it. I have no clue where this theory came from, but it makes a ton of sense, looking back at my past and how I handled things. I was always told that I wasn't good enough, so I didn't want to find someone who I *KNEW* was better than me as I was scared to hear it from them.

I did try to level up . . .

My theory came out to be tested when I dated a guy who I thought had it all. Someone who was my idea of a level up from me. Uneven playing grounds! I took the plunge to try it out and see how I felt. Well, in this relationship I felt like I had to change myself to better myself for him. He told me to dress different, or that I needed to look the way he wanted. So I felt very self-conscious about it, thinking I wasn't good enough for him. His reason for breaking up with me was that I was not "hot enough" for him. This destroyed me . . . I found out a couple years later I was never going to be hot enough for him, as it finally came out that he played for the other team. He was gay. It made a ton of sense as, looking back, I could see some red flags but chose to ignore it. It still was a really shitty feeling going through that and hearing that I was not good enough for him. (More on this in Chapter 3).

I have been learning that you are good enough just as you are. You can laugh at your own jokes, even when no one is laughing. Trust me, they will laugh too, if you are laughing. It is one of my favourite things; to tell something I think is funny and to laugh right after makes my heart grow. But before, I was always nervous to say something in case I was looked at like, *Why would she say that? That is dumb* . . . I have done a lot of assuming in my life about how people see me and what they think of me. I have a terrible gremlin living in my head that has made me feel pretty shitty for a lot of my life. But I am working towards a better me. Getting all of this out has really helped me heal and move forward, instead of pushing it down as though none of it happened. I highly encourage you to write things down that bother you, or get your story out on paper, even if it goes nowhere, this process has been life changing for me.

"Strength does not come from winning. Your struggles develop your strengths. When you go through hardships and decide not to surrender, that is strength"

—Mohandas Gandhi

CHAPTER 2

A CRY FOR HELP

✳ Trigger Warning: Topic of Suicide ✳

"Everything we do is either an act of love or a cry for help."

–Marianne Williamson

This is another heavy topic that I think we need to absolutely talk more about with people—not just teens, but anyone who is suffering. They need to know it is okay to reach out and ask for help. It is okay to be suffering—most people are not okay. However, it is so great to see that it is becoming more normalized to talk about. Just because you are suffering doesn't make you any less of a person.

I believe that we all have our own ways of crying for help. A lot of times we are too scared we are going to get in trouble for what happened, judged or looked at differently. We hide the truth or avoid talking about it. Deep down we want to talk about it, but we might not know how to bring it up. I think it is hardest for kids to talk about these things because they literally have no control over their lives; they have to answer to their parents and deal with the reactions that come from sharing. Do you have any idea how terrifying it is to talk about how you are feeling when you are a kid? I know some kids are extroverts and they can share easily but introverts, holy! It is hard!! I am one of those people. Sharing feelings is really hard. I have two extremes—either I share things like word vomit, that usually are more about things going on in my life than how I am feeling, or I completely shut down and try to push everyone away and I just keep it inside. I am a bottler. I try to focus on anyone else rather than confront my feelings.

Knowing this was the type of kid I was, I tried to find other ways to get the pain out. I tried to write in a diary how I was feeling but to be honest I just couldn't get it down on paper. I wrote mostly superficial, high level things, like, "Today at school we did this in math and then at lunch we walked to Tim Hortons." Oh, and I had to throw something in there about my crush to make it a legit diary entry. I FELT like I had to write this stuff down. That is what girls write about, isn't it? There is no way other girls felt the way I was feeling. I was the only one, had to be. I guess a part of me was scared that someone was going to read my diary and they would find things out I didn't want them to know about.

The Bright Side

Because of the feeling of needing to write things down, I later figured out that I really enjoyed writing. I wrote poems to start; I have put a few in this book, in Chapter 10. They were mostly sad, sappy ones about a boy or how a boy hurt me. Real good teenage boy drama stuff. Eventually, I got into writing stories. I would use the computer time I was given at home to write my stories. I would save them on floppy disks (anyone born after the 1990s probably won't even know what this is—think of a USB stick flattened out and in the shape of a square. We had to put them in the computer and then try not to lose them when they were in our hand). Once I was done writing, I always printed it out on brightly coloured paper. I don't know why we even had those bright colours. And by bright, I am talking highlighter green, yellow and orange. I think deep down I printed them on this coloured paper so that if someone found it, the colour would catch their eye and maybe they'd read them. I think deep down I wanted someone to read them, to see I was hurting.

My stories would be "made up" and about someone else, but in actual fact they were about my feelings, my thoughts, and sometimes things that happened to me. But I never admitted that to anyone. I didn't want them to know it was me. It was just me putting words to paper about things that are in the movies. I used to watch a lot of killer, crime, action movies and rarely the romantic chick flicks. Want to know why? I thought the likelihood of those romantic things happening were slim to none for me. So I watched the slasher movies. I sometimes thought, *I just wish something like this would happen to me so then it all would be over.* I wished for something bad to happen to me, so that I wouldn't have to hurt anymore. I wanted to be dead. Can you believe I felt that dying was going to be better than living my life? Pretty sad for someone who just wanted to make a difference in the world.

The Pain We Put Ourselves Through . . .

When I was sad or hurting I would think of ways I could hurt myself. I would think things like what it would be like if all of a sudden a car crashed into my car or if I drove off a cliff. I remember one time I was camping with my family and I was upset. I don't remember why, but it had to do with my boyfriend at the time. It was either that I had the time to think about things as I was with my family and not him, or we'd had a fight about something, but I'd had enough and I was ready to end this.

I was walking to the lake while crying so hard. I made a point to walk off the trail in the bushes to avoid bumping into anyone. It was nighttime as well—I'm not sure how I was able to go out by myself in the dark, but it happened. I quickly came up with the plan that I was going to just go into the lake and keep walking until I could not touch anymore and then just sink. My plan was to basically just walk in to the water and have it wash over me and then just black out. I had planned to go in with my clothes on and just walk until I could not walk anymore. I really don't know at this point why this was my idea. I think it was all that I could come up with since I was not at home. Thinking back, though, I don't believe my plan would have worked for many reasons. One of them being that I was scared to put my head under the water.

I always figured if things were in my head and no one knew how I was feeling, then it would be easier to end things than if someone was trying to stop me. I want to tell you about another one of my terrible nights that I can remember from my past. It is a night I will never forget, it was the night that my mom found out how I was feeling.

I don't remember the actual reason for why I was feeling this way, or how we even got to the moment that replays in my head every time I hear the word suicide. Replaying it back it feels like I was in this trance and I remember nothing until the very tip of the memory that was the most raw, intense, heartbreaking moment. I don't believe that my mom and I discussed it ever again. With the recent suicide attempts of my stepdaughter and other young teens in the community, this topic has become a real tough one to talk about. I have had to share my story with my stepdaughter, and I was almost in tears when I told it.

The Night I Thought Would be the End

I am sitting on the bathroom floor. As I look down through the tears in my eyes, I see my wrist parallel to a razor blade. My shaking hand, my disbelief in what I am seeing. My mom sitting on the other side of the locked door, crying and screaming at me to let her in and to not hurt myself. The pain that is screaming out of her and my heart breaking. In this moment I know that if she got in here and saw me lying on the floor bleeding out, she would be devastated. She is making every effort to get into this tiny room to save me. To show me she loves me, to show me that I don't have to do this and I just can't unlock that door . . . I don't want to see her disappointed, crying face and hear the words she might say to me. The words that will basically make me feel like the biggest disappointment in the world. Feeling selfish because I just do not want to feel like this anymore.

Something kept me from letting her in and I think deep down it was that I didn't know how to move on from there. The pain I was feeling was so deep that I thought nothing she said was going to open the door. Something did, however, got me to open that door finally. I have no idea how long I was in there, but my mom NEVER gave up, she NEVER left the door, she wasn't going to stop talking, not even for a second. And I think even though I couldn't hear what she was saying, or I didn't want to hear it, her presence at the door was enough to make me realize I wasn't alone. That someone would care if I was not there. Someone would be hurting more than I was if I went through with this. So I opened the door and I let her hold me. I cried and cried until I just couldn't anymore.

To this day, I feel like this has been hanging over me for putting my mom through this. It hurts me to know that I am the one who put her in that terrible moment. But I will always be grateful that she never left me alone, because the outcome might be a lot different. So, Mom, if you are reading this . . . thank you so much for not leaving me, and I am so sorry I put you through that, but thank you for not giving up on me.

"The struggle you're in today is developing the strength you need tomorrow."

—Robert Tew

Fear of Water

Growing up, I had tubes put in my ears because I was getting a lot of ear infections. One of the ears was totally fine, the other was not. The tubes that were put in ended up causing a hole in my ear drum. So I spent most of my teenage years having surgeries on my ear drum and recovering for weeks afterwards. They first used a type of cloth material, which didn't hold; they tried again with the same material, which also didn't hold. The final time, they actually cut open my ear from the back and used the cartilage to fix the hole. The third time seemed to be the winner! However, I hated swimming; I hated going to the pool, and I hated putting my head under the water, even in the shower. I had to wear one of those swimming caps. You know those ones that grandmas usually wear swimming laps at the pool? Yeah, those. It was so embarrassing. So I just chose not to go under the water—still, to this day, I hate putting my head under.

A Scary Moment

My biggest worry was that the hole in my ear would open again because of the pressure under the water. My fear grew even more when my boyfriend at the time thought it would be funny to hold me underwater. We were at the river and went swimming, just the two of us. He thought it would be really funny if he came up to me like he was going to hug me and shoot up in the water to push me down into the water and hold me there. I have never been so panicked up until that point in my life. A part of me thought he might drown me, because of the abuse he had shown me before. I was scared he wasn't going to let me above water. He finally let me up and just laughed and told me he was joking. Ever since this day, any time I go under water I panic. My heart races, I feel like I can't breathe. I am talking about even when I go snorkeling. That is the closest activity I will do to see the fish. I could not do scuba diving. No way. I feel I would panic and not be able to do it.

Don't Turn Your Back to Water

I remember going on a family vacation to Hawaii and my current boyfriend was with us. It was the first big trip he had come on and I am not sure he understood my fear of being under water. The waves scare me; I hate going in the water when they are big. I remember as a kid I was swimming with my mom and my cousins out in the water. We were kind of wave riding, or just getting past it. A huge wave came and I panicked because I didn't know what to do. I let the wave crash on me instead of diving into it. I always thought I could just get above that wake and I could make it over. Well, nope. I didn't make it and I didn't want my mom to see me freaked out so I quickly got out and didn't go back in again that day.

So this trip I was trying to test out my wave riding skills so he wouldn't think I was a wuss. My boyfriend wanted to go in the water and so I braved it. I was able to get out past the crashing waves without an issue just a fast heartbeat. Coming in . . . well that was a different story. I decided to go back to shore, as I was getting tired of treading water, but I decided to go at the worst time. Big waves came crashing down on me and I felt like I could not get up. I felt like I was being held down, an instant flashback to when my ex-boyfriend had held me underwater.

When I finally got above the water I had a massive panic attack. This was the first time my boyfriend witnessed one of these start to finish. I got out quick and ran down the beach. My family didn't understand it. They had no idea what was wrong with me. They just told my boyfriend to go deal with me. I could not breathe, I couldn't catch my breath to even stop running. He got out and yelled after me but had no idea what had happened. I explained to him and he kind of understood. He didn't know about my past experience with being held under water. Fifteen plus years later and I am still scared to be underwater.

Even Adults Think About It...

Even in adulthood, I still think about what it would be like to just end things. When I get so stressed, overwhelmed, or have a really bad anxiety attack, I think to myself, *Who would be sad if I was gone? Would it make things simpler?* Sometimes it shows up when I am driving and I think, I could easily just go off that cliff or swerve into on coming traffic. I don't act on the feelings, but I shouldn't be feeling this way. No one should. As adults we have different stresses than we did when we were kids, but they seem so much bigger because other people depend on you. As a kid you just expect your parents will save you, and you are more worried about what others think of you rather than how anyone else is feeling around you.

"Sometimes we truly begin to find ourselves when we are so broken & weak ... and in that moment a spark ignites & we dig down & find the strength to stand strong & fight on."

—Kim Bayne

CHAPTER 3

ONLINE "DATING"

✳ Trigger Warning: Topic around Rape ✳

"Online dating is efficient. We're a fast food society and now you have a pool of eligible people to choose from."

—Gail Barsky

Online. Dating. Yep that is what the world has come to. No more are the days where you meet your person in public. When you meet randomly in public, you would spend the time being yourself because you just randomly meet this person and they know nothing about you. Nothing to hide and no one to try to compete with, you had their full attention. Now we have to post our best photo, Photoshopped or not, you decide. Write about all the best things about you and what you enjoy—or lie. Some people just straight up lie. Then you have to swipe right or left depending if you like them or not off of first glance. Some apps require the females to speak to the males first, some apps the computer matches you and you decide if you want to talk to them.

Depending on how you answer the questions, that is who you get matched with, someone who is similar to you. Some apps you pay for, some you do not. Honestly, I have tried both ways and both are just as terrible. Mind you, some people still meet in person through friends, or still the magic of one stranger to another. There are not many people I know who have had success that way, but there still is hope!

We All Experience It

When I moved to Edmonton in 2015 I had two roommates that just wanted to get out and date in the new city. So what was the easiest way to meet guys? Well, online of course. We all downloaded Tinder—most popular app at the time. I ended up keeping it for a couple days, then deleted it. My one roommate seemed to swipe right to almost everyone and had quite a few first dates at our house. One guy I remember came over a few times and after he left, our fair skinned roommate would have a couple new hickeys all over her. I guess that was part of their hang out time activities.

She had a guy come over on New Years Eve, and she ended up getting so drunk early in the night, she got sick in the bathroom while he sat in the living room. #FirstDateFail.

She did end up meeting this one guy on there and he stuck around. Our lease was up and we all kind of decided to go our own ways; my roommate didn't really look for a place, so when the time was up she ended up moving in with the Tinder guy. Fast forward to present day: They are parents of two beautiful children and working on a future together. They are one of the success stories of online dating

Ghosting is a thing . . .

Once I lived on my own after we went our separate ways, I was feeling pretty lonely, so I tried the app again. I matched with a couple of guys. This was the first time I was free to do whatever I wanted and date whoever because I didn't have anyone living with me; I didn't have anyone to answer to. You know that feeling of needing permission to do things, or not wanting the other person to feel left out. I'd feel bad bringing a guy into our space as well, especially when you share a space with two others. I did have a couple of guys that came to the house but I knew them because bringing them over.

I met this one guy who was really nice but had a bad boy side to him. As I got to know him more, the nice part of him didn't stick around. He never wanted to sleep over; he never once came to my house, always made me go to his—which was a half hour each way. Eventually he ghosted me.

** *Ghosting, also known as simmering or icing, is a colloquial term which describes the practice of ending all communication and contact with another person without any apparent warning or justification and subsequently ignoring any attempts to reach out or communication made by said person . . . The term originated in the early 2000s, typically refer-ring to dating and romantic relationships. In the following decade, media reported a rise in ghosting, which has been attributed to the increasing use of social media and online dating apps.* ** *(Wikipedia. n.d.)*

He just stopped returning my calls and texts, so then I got really mad and upset. Put a huge amount of self-guilt in my head. I blamed myself for him not wanting me. Then I analyzed everything I said and did. Never could figure it out. Why is ghosting someone okay?

Another online dating horror was after I was seeing a guy that I met through my best friend at the time. I really liked this guy and he wanted nothing to do with dating me, just having fun. He was so focused on anything other than dating, and I admired him for it, part of why I liked him. He had goals and dreams. However, it did not go in my favour because I had to see him all the time after that and I still liked him! Anyways, I was upset and wanted someone to take my mind of this guy, so I downloaded Tinder again. This time I found a guy who was just down the road from me; he wasn't looking for anything serious, just someone to hang out with as he was new to town. Or so he told me. He wasn't a big texter so he told me if I wanted to get to know him, come over and hang out.

So I decided, *Okay, sure.* When I got to his house I found out it was in the basement, but you had to go through the upstairs house to get there. It was pretty weird. It was a dark dungeon-like space. He just told me to sit wherever; he was going to go to the bathroom. He turned the corner and left the door open as he peed. I was like, *This is so not what I was picturing.* We watched a movie, and then I told him I was going to go home. He begged me to stay, and I said no. I went home.

A couple nights later he asked me to come back over. He said he actually doesn't have a car or license and he doesn't like to go out with girls without a car. I agreed to meet him at his house again. This time I made him cookies—was trying to be nice, I guess. When I got there he told me we should go to the liquor store. So we did and then we got back to his house. He was acting a bit weird. I found out he was doing cocaine any moment he could, but not in front of me.

This random guy showed up, and they did a hit together. After that he just did it openly in front of me. Told me only cool people do it and I was missing out. *Yeah, no thanks.* I had not done any drugs in my life and was not starting now. He made me feel bad for not doing it. He told me that he was going to bed and I better be following him. I sat on the couch for a moment. *What do I do?* I really wanted to go home, but at the same time I didn't really want to sleep alone.

I stayed. What a mistake that was . . .

As soon as we got into bed he forced himself on me. Told me, "Shhhh, shhh, shhh, it'll be okay." He slowly tried to get me excited and then he said, "Ah fuck it." Lifted me up, threw me onto my back closer to the edge, flipped me over, held my arms behind my back and started pushing himself on me. I was telling him no, I don't want to. He yelled at me to shut up, it would be quick. I was lying there crying as he got back into bed and fell asleep. He was snoring. I was still lying there, and I just wanted to get out. I got up and picked up all my stuff and left.

I got the hell out of there. I cried the entire way home and continued until I fell asleep on the couch. What a terrible feeling. When I woke up two hours later, I felt disgusting. I was in pain, felt gross, exhausted. I decided to have a bath to get the feeling off of me. It didn't really help. Nothing helps when someone does this to you. They take something from you. It's a feeling you never shake. Nothing makes it come off of your skin because it is embedded in you. It took me a while to want to do anything but hide in my house. I didn't even tell anyone this had happened because I blamed myself for being in that situation when my gut had told me not to do it. I don't even remember if I told anyone where I was. Things could have gone a lot worse.

Looking back, I see all of the red flags that I did not see or want to see at the time. I just wanted the attention, I guess, which is not a great reason. I put my morals and judgements aside to hang out with someone who was NOT worth my time or energy. That is partly why I blame myself for what happened. I should never have let myself get to that point. I should have just moved on as soon as I saw the first red flag. Why did I think giving my time to someone who clearly had no desire to even think about my feelings was worth it? My self confidence was low and it felt like every guy I dated would make me feel as though I was worthless. I never thought I would be able to have a really good guy in my life because I didn't deserve it. Everyone I dated made me feel that way anyways.

Read Between the Lines

Needless to say, I stopped online dating and tried to date friends of friends. That turned out interesting, but that is a different story.

I had given up on the dating scene, but one night I was with my friend and she was telling me about her online dating situation and how she had ended up finding a really good guy (or so we thought in the beginning). Then I felt I needed to revisit it. I was feeling pretty defeated at this point and felt like I should just like the people I totally didn't think were anywhere near my league on the good looking scale. I was absolutely shocked, then, when this really good looking guy was interested in me. He swiped right!

It took me a while to figure out what to say to him, and he didn't send me a message, so I sent him one before I went to bed. In the morning I woke up and quickly looked at my phone to see if he had responded; he hadn't. I figured he wouldn't. I went on with my day and then I got home from work. He had sent me a message back. We talked a bit that night, and then the next day we decided to make plans. He came over to my house and when I opened the door I was like, *Whoa, he is even better looking in person than in his pictures.* We had a great time talking and then he went home. We continued talking and hanging out; I felt pretty lucky because he was so nice and good looking and wanted to be with me. As we started hanging out more, we would go out with his friends or spend time with his family. Red flags kept popping up but I ignored them. He always wanted to go out to the country bar and dance—and rightfully so, as he was a great dancer. He was the complete opposite of most guys; he wasn't pressuring me to have sex or anything.

Things started to get a bit weird after about a month. He made me come to his place all of the time; I think he had only been to my place once or twice. Never did he sleep over. It was farther for me to go to work if I stayed at his place, but I was happy, so I dealt with it. He didn't really like PDA or kissing too much. He didn't like to do anything that I wanted to do, or hang out with my friends. He started telling me that if he didn't like my outfit I wasn't supposed to wear it again, or told me how I could make it better. He would rate how I looked by how he would describe me. Cute, pretty, comfy, etc. He told me things he wanted me to change like go get red lipstick and wear it every time he saw me. I just chalked it up to him trying to help me with my style, since I didn't really have a specific style.

My mom and sister came to visit me and were able to meet him. My mom instantly loved him, then my sister did too after my mom gave approval. Side note—my family never liked any of my boyfriends. They would accept them for the most part, but they didn't enjoy them being around. So I was very excited I finally got approval!

I got pretty close with his sister and cousin, and then found out details that really were concerning; the biggest one was that he had never had a relationship over three months. That was a big flag for me.

We had plans for our three month anniversary to go to a Luke Bryan concert. One of my favs! So I was thinking, *Oh this is going to go past three months for sure then!*

About two weeks beforehand, he started being pretty distant. When we hung out on the weekend he didn't really want to do much, and he went to bed early and left me up with his roommate. One morning he kicked me out early, as he had stuff to do, apparently. Then he up and disappeared for an entire week. I was stressed out, thinking, *What is going on, where is he?* He finally texted me and told me he was helping his sister move and was just too busy to talk to me. Then he asked to call me. That was the nail in the coffin. I knew what was coming. He called to tell me that he'd spent time away from me and didn't miss me at all. He said that I just didn't fit into his life right and that I wasn't hot enough to be by his side.

Wow . . . this was a huge blow to me. I'd thought we were good. He'd asked me to be his girlfriend on my birthday. He knew my birthdays always ended in tears, so he wanted to do something nice for me. His birthday was the day before mine and we did a super-hero themed night—it had been so fun! I was finally happy and then this . . . devastating. Then when I realized that we were literally a couple days away from three months, I got it. I understood. I was pretty sad to be missing out on the Luke Bryan concert. And then I found out he had taken someone else, and that stung even more. Needless to say, I don't listen to Luke Bryan anymore.

The Positive Side

I try to look at every relationship with some positive aspect, or learning for next time, although the learning part doesn't tend to stick! One thing that ended up helping me in the future was the fact that he had been celiac, and I had to learn all about that. A few years later I ended up finding out I had a gluten intolerance so it made it easier to switch to a gluten free lifestyle knowing that I saw him do it, and it didn't seem as hard as I thought. The negative side of things is that after he broke up with me like that, I started to second guess myself on everything. My style, my clothes, my hair, my make up—everything. I felt like I had NO idea who I was.

I don't know if you can tell or not, but I let other people affect me so much that I have questioned who I am. The hardest part is hearing from all my relationships that I was not good enough, or I was not the dream girl or whatever form it came in. It is really hard to not take this to heart when you rarely heard good things about yourself. I made the mistake of letting people control my feelings and emotions, and for what?!

About a year or two later I decided to just see what he was up to—you know, the good old social media stalking of your ex . . . we all do it, don't deny it! I came across his profile and found out that he had come out that he was gay. Which I think is amazing, and it actually made me feel a lot better, because there was no way I would ever be hot enough for him. That was why he was trying to change me, because I wasn't what he actually wanted, and he just didn't know it at the time, or didn't want to admit it. It is really hard to date someone who doesn't know what team they play for.

As females, we second guess or blame ourselves for not being what the guy wants. So many things made sense after finding this information out. I felt like I could move past it. It was no longer anything I could blame myself for.

Another Go

Later in life, after a break up and my mom getting cancer for the second time, I tried out the app again (I know, I know, I should have just given up on it, as nothing good had come out of dating online!). I had just moved back to the Westcoast after ending a long-term relationship, and was trying to figure out my life and self again. This relationship had sucked the life right out of me and it was very toxic. I decided one night I was going to give myself thirty minutes on Tinder, and if nothing came of it, delete it and move on. Minute twenty-eight minutes, and bam, you have a match. I am not going to lie to you, I totally swiped right on his picture not thinking I would get a swipe back. He was a babe and his eyes were incredible. We spent the night texting back and forth, and continued on for four days. We spoke on the phone and talked as much as we could. He was open with me about his past and his present situation with his kids. It was a lot of information to take in, and by no means an easy situation.

On the fifth day I was heading out of town to visit my sister, and I was waiting at my gate for my flight when I got a text saying, "Hey, are you already through security?" I said yes, I was. He said, "Come outside the gate." I was freaking out! He was there! I hadn't met him yet, and I was so nervous to come out of security and see him. I walked out and there he was, with flowers. He gave me the biggest hug and he was blushing and smiling so much. It was the absolute best feeling. But then I overstayed my time on the other side of security and ended up missing my flight, and what was supposed to be a one hour flight turned into a four hour trip with a layover. Needless to say, my family wasn't too excited! But they couldn't wait to hear why I had missed my flight. I will never forget the first time I met him, as it was probably the best first meeting I have ever had.

"Sometimes you just have to die a little inside in order to be reborn and rise again as a stronger and wiser version of you."

–Unknown

CHAPTER 4

INVISIBLE SCARS

✵ Trigger Warning: Anxiety/Mental Health ✵

Note to Self: I don't have to take this day all at once, but rather, one step, one breath, one moment at a time. I am only one person. Things will get done when they get done.

Natalie Frost

I didn't grow up with anxiety; it came later in life. Like a big airplane crashing into land, pieces of it going flying. I remember I was twenty-five years old, which felt like a big year for me in general. Not really sure why, as most people think the big years are thirty, forty, fifty, etc. No half decades. BUT to me, twenty-five kind of felt like now you are a legit adult. Up until this time it felt like I was still a kid and could do whatever and it would be okay.

When I was twenty-five I was living in a new city, new job, new home, working three jobs, away from my family and most of my friends. It was a lot of change and a lot of new stressors. And then BAM out of nowhere I got hit extremely hard with an anxiety attack. At the time I had no idea what it was. I remember it pretty vividly, although I don't remember WHY I had the attack. I was sitting at my desk at work and all of a sudden my heart started racing, my palms got sweaty, and I could feel the tears about to roll down my cheeks. I quickly got up and basically ran to the bathroom, which of course was on the other side of the office. I slammed the door shut in the stall and sat on the ground sobbing, trying to slow my heart rate down and trying to get a deep breath in. This was one of the moments where you aren't sure how to make this weird sensation stop. Then you start to get scared, like what if you can't stop crying or breathing quickly? What if you pass out from hyperventilating?

Imagine, you are at work, sitting there minding your own business and then bam out of nowhere this anxiety creature hits you like a slap in the face. Stuns you from knowing what the hell to do. The other problem—you didn't bring your phone, so you can't even text your friend to come help you. You are truly alone. Alone with your thoughts and alone with this creature that you need to tame.

The longest thirty minutes go by and finally you are able to calm down. You go to the sink and see your face is a mess and your cheeks are red. Take the time to clean yourself up the best you can, breathe one more time. Walk out with your head high, hoping no one from your office saw or heard anything.

> *"Stress and anxiety at work have less to do with the work we do and more to do with weak management and leadership."*
>
> —Simon Sinek

One of Those Times

Imagine you are living your life every day as you normally would, until bam you feel like you can't breathe. Your heart is jumping out of your chest, your breathing has gotten quicker, you can't speak, body trembling, tears rolling down your cheeks. Not only do you have no idea what is happening to you, but you are freaking out, wondering who is watching you. How the hell do I make this stop? *That is all you can focus on right now.*

Anxiety can cripple you, it can take down even the strongest people. It is not an easy battle to win and it can consume you. Finding the help you need while trying to live a "normal" life is really difficult. Most days it is hard to even want to get up, pretending that everything is okay. Scared of when the next attack might happen.

Breathe. Deep breaths. Focus on the breath. It is going to be okay. Breathe. Loosen your body from the grip. Breathe. Trying to repeat this in your head is hard; it is a lot easier when someone is around to help you repeat it. The hardest part is knowing the signs of when an attack will occur; no one can see the pain on the inside, and the outside looks the same. Don't let someone you love suffer in silence.

To this day, anxiety seems to just come out of the woodwork when it is least wanted. Before a big test, meeting new people, starting something new, getting yelled at, making a mistake, being a step-parent, etc. Literally this creature jumps at you at your worst time. Luckily for the people who are going through this, we no longer have to feel alone. There are so many resources you can find to help you with these feelings. There are apps you can have on your phone, like Headspace, a great app to help with meditation, sleep, and proper breathing. There is a great book called *Dare* by Barry McDonagh, as well he has an app called Dare, similar to Headspace but more about how to get over the anxiety as a whole.

There is a great inspirational quote by Barry McDonagh on the Dare app:

"There are millions of perfectly sane, normal people who have the exact same problem as you."

I like this quote because it makes you see that you are not broken, you are not worthless, and you are not a terrible person. There are so many other people going through the same thing; it has just not been widely talked about. The support that is out there now is amazing; you can get medication to help, tools such as apps, books, courses, etc. Just don't give up. You can do this, you can get through it. Just don't be scared to talk about it or to ask for help.

I Knew I Wasn't Alone

One of my longest friends has had anxiety in her life since grade 7. The creature arrived when she had to get up and do a speech. Most people hate public speaking BUT when anxiety comes a knockin' it makes it extra hard. It was her turn to do her speech in front of the class. They hadn't done too much preparing the students for public speaking, so she was really nervous. She was up at the podium, started to speak, not thinking anything of being scared or stressing over it, and then BOOM! Anxiety. Her voice changed. She couldn't move. She lost her breath and went all tingly. She ended up having to sit down and focus on her breath. Needless to say, that is not the most comfortable situation to occur in front of your whole class. Later on into high school, anxiety just got worse. It would sneak up on her in class when she was just sitting there! On a few occasions she actually passed out because she was not breathing properly. It turned into an extra morning routine, where the anxiety creature would come out in the morning before school and make it very hard for her to eat. Because this became a life crippling issue, her mom took her to the doctor to see what they could do to help. They threw a Band-Aid on the issue with anti-anxiety or anti-depression medications. But that Band-Aid turned her into a robot and then with that, she became suicidal.

After reading *Dare* by Barry McDonagh, I lent her my book to see if it could help her with her creature. I asked her what the one thing was that stuck out for her, which helped her move forward with life. Her response was giving your anxiety a name and talking to it as though it is a visitor and won't be staying long. She has named her creature Penny. I asked her why Penny. She said, "I call her Penny, like the coin, because anxiety comes and it makes no sense as to why it is here. A penny coin is worth a cent. So no senses and one cent makes sense and that is how Penny was born."

A Recommendation

I suggest writing down what happened with your first anxiety attack as soon as you are past it; what did it feel like? What were you doing? How were you right before the attack? What symptoms came up for you? How did you end the attack? How did you feel afterwards? It can be extremely draining mentally, emotionally, and sometimes physically. Acknowledging the emotions and what took place can sometimes help you move past it and not stress about the next one, because you can and will get past it.

Sometimes the attacks don't make any sense at all. One of my friends started having issues in grade 9. Her first memory of her anxiety creature coming out was in Science class; she got dizzy, sweaty, felt like her heard was buzzing, and her stomach was killing her. She felt she couldn't tell anyone or even explain it, so she would just tell people her stomach hurt when she was bored. Which in fact was when most of her attacks happened, unprovoked in the middle of class. She had no idea it was her anxiety creature until she went to her doctor and explained what she was going through. She spent most of high school with Ativan constantly on hand and the only thing that stops her attacks to this day is Ativan, or calling her mom. Hearing her mom's voice causes the creature to calm down. She does not have an anxiety trigger like some people; hers are completely random.

Now You Add in Random Attacks

How is one supposed to deal with random attacks!? It comes down to finding the tools that help calm the creature down. Everyone is different, and everyone has their own stories. If you have anxiety or even if you do not, ask one of your friends if they do and get them to explain it to you. It is eye opening.

Breathe. Deep breaths. Breathe. You can get past this.

Sometimes, anxiety attacks can actually open your eyes to things that you may have missed otherwise. I had a really bad attack during the time I was writing the book and I actually wrote a blurb about it post-attack:

> *I have never wanted to focus on my breathing, I didn't think that would matter. We breathe every day without thinking about it, so why do I need to focus on it? I tried all these things like meditation, yoga, breathing deeply, courses, seminars, and I still just didn't get it. I thought I was doing things right but I felt no better. I also didn't understand what amazing healing powers nature has for you. Lately I have been going into nature to calm my anxiety and to get fresh air. I think we all take advantage of the beauty around us and I didn't really focus on what the beauty can do for you. Until today. Deep breathing is so important to calm down your system and doing a few deep breaths in nature helps that much more. The smell of nature, the beauty all around and just the fresh air helps give your lungs a big hug.*

In the Moment

I am currently coming down from a really intense anxiety attack. I don't have these often but when I do, watch out, you have no idea how long they will last as I can't control it. I'm not here to talk about what caused my anxiety attack; I want to focus on the response I had.

I knew an anxiety attack was coming; I could feel the tears building and my heart pounding and my breathing speeding up. My instinct was to go to my bathroom. I was crying nonstop so I couldn't see very well. I sat cross legged in the middle of the room and rocked back and forth, back and forth, while wiping away my tears.

I had my eyes closed and instantly I had a reminder pop into my head about an app I've been listening to for meditation. They had something for feeling overwhelmed, I remembered. I opened up Headspace and quickly found the "Feeling Overwhelmed 3 minute meditation." I thought yeah right, three minutes? I don't think I'll be calmed down but let's try.

So I clicked "Start" and closed my eyes with tears running down . . . I was breathing through my mouth as I zoned out and realized I wasn't calming down. Then I noticed I was breathing through my nose only, so I took a big breathe in through my nose and out through my mouth. It felt different? It felt better! I took two more and I stopped my tears, I did two more and the audio stopped. I had my eyes still closed and I took one last breath and opened my eyes to the view of my shower curtain that has big forest trees on it; the rug on the floor was a rock pattern. I felt calmer in this room because it looked like I was in the forest. I have also learned that walking in the forest instantly helps calm my anxiety.

"You are not a weak or cowardly person for having an anxiety problem."

—Barry McDonagh, *Dare: The New Way to End Anxiety and Stop Panic Attacks Fast*

CHAPTER 5

STEPPARENTING . . .
WHERE DO I BEGIN . . .

"A good stepmom is not made—she is built. She is built by the hardships of her role, the tears she cried in secret, and by the lessons she learns through trial and error."

—Unknown

"The passionate stepmom lives in all of us. She makes mistakes. She has strong opinions that she often can't express. She remains quiet when she wants to scream. She makes sacrifices others may not be capable of. She learns how to love in many different ways. And she gives. She gives her heart, her soul, and her life to making sure a child she didn't give birth to smiles, has wonderful memories, and—most importantly—feels loved."

—The Blended Truth, Blended Family consulting

This. Is. The. Hardest. Job. Ever. You are taken for granted and the appreciation is not shown often by your step kids. You also don't really have any legal say or anything in that matter, and that can be really frustrating. You don't get to pick where the kids go to day care, or activities, or the disciplinary actions. You basically have to abide by the rules of the mother of said kid. Forget being celebrated on Mother's Day or sometimes your birthday because you are usually an afterthought for them. My stepdaughter is the worst for showing me any sort of celebration. She will hide in her room all day, or when I do see her she just glares and refuses to say "Happy Birthday," and on Mother's Day she just ignores it like it doesn't exist. My stepson always says "Happy Birthday" or "Happy stepmom's day." But it feels like the teen ruins that in the end, and God forbid we do what I want on those days.

There can be a lot of baggage in these relationships that you may not know about until later. You may have kids involved with different parents, so then you get to deal with more than one ex of your partner's past. There is also the potential for court, mediation, child support, spousal support, etc. Once you move in together, your money is no longer YOUR money. Also, forget having any space or anything of yours. My stepdaughter just goes into my room or office and takes what she wants. She will go through my purse and not care it is not hers. At one point, I found out she was borrowing my underwear!!!

But The Reward...

BUT it can also be really rewarding at times. Like when they tell you they love you, or they ask you to hang out with them. It took my stepdaughter two years before she would even consider giving me a hug. They are very few and far between, but it is a step forward and she is not a big hugger in general. When you get to go to their important events, they see you are so proud of them and they smile at you, knowing damn well they are glad you are there.

I also find that with a teenage stepchild I am able to have a relationship with her that is important for her to openly share with me and get things off her chest. She has a lot in her head and has not had the best track record for reliable, safe adults in her life where she didn't feel judged or told she is lying. Sometimes I do not want to hear what she is telling me, but in that moment, I know it is to help her and she has no one else to talk to. She trusts me and I try every day to make sure I don't break that trust. But when she breaks my trust, it hurts a lot. It can be taken very hard. Does she say she cares? Nope. Whether she does or doesn't, hearing that hurts. Especially when you put everything into her and plan your day/life around her.

Unpredictable

Being a stepparent, you can't predict how it will be, no one relationship is the same. My relationship with my step kids, and the one I had with my partner's ex, was actually pretty good, until something happened and now we no longer have contact with his ex directly. We have to go through a third party to get any information. However, on the plus side, I don't have to deal with a high maintenance ex that wants to go to court all the time. I have no idea what she says about me to her son but I do hear about what the grandmother says to people about me and to the kids. Spreading lies and assumptions ruined the relationship I was trying to have with her. I tried to get her to see her grandson as much as possible because he was missing her, but then she caused a really terrible situation, and I no longer wanted to have her anywhere near my life. Her loss.

Having a part of the family against you while trying to figure out this difficult relationship balance, where you aren't acting like you are trying to take the mother role, or to put rules in place to be a dictator—you basically walk on egg shells all the time. Mind you the beginning of the relationship was the best, getting to know the kids and learning how to make them enjoy time with you. You know, *the fun part*. Then that stage disappears and no matter what you do, you just are the enemy once they become teenagers.

NATALIE FROST

Respect is Not Given by the Teen

Speaking from my personal experience, respect is not given at all by a step teen when you come into their life late. You will get the eye rolls, the ignored times, the rude times, the disrespect constantly, and then you hope for at least a couple days in there where you can breathe and get some energy for the next thing to come along. Typically I am lucky to get two days in a row without an issue, but then she is usually up to something, like going through my things and stealing my phone and hiding it. We have had to get the police involved with some situations. She has also gone to the hospital a couple times for suicidal thoughts. It is never a dull day with a teenager.

As I said before, this is not the case for everyone; some families figure it out and the kids treat the other adults as bonus people in their life. I am not sure how those people got so lucky to be in that situation but man would that be easier than this.

Generation Z

This generation of teenagers have so much to struggle with; having a broken family does not help. Especially when they just want to be like everyone else. My teen tries to compare herself to other teens, but she is not like everyone else. She has had experiences that more than likely her peers have not had. Some days are much worse than others, where I find a spot to just cry and hope that one of them doesn't see me. There are some days it feels absolutely shitty and lonely while also second guessing myself a lot. I have been told by teachers, counselors, social workers, and other parents that this is just normal for this generation. Which makes it even sadder that we are just accepting that this is "normal."

Mental health and suicide rates are rising, and are now even worse with COVID. Kids are starting to be sexually active as young as grades 5-6, and drugs are also involved at this age. A young girl in my community who just turned twelve was at a sleep over and overdosed from heroin. At twelve. Middle school kids are drug dealers, fifteen- to sixteen-year-olds are having erectile dysfunction because they started watching porn so young that they can't finish the act unless they whip out their cell phones and watch porn while having sex. I would be so devastated being a girl who had to go through that. I don't even want to think about what bad self talk would be happening in the girls head.

The other piece is that some teens think that rough sex is "normal"; that includes choking each other which is really scary . . . I remember when I was younger we would play this game where we would try to choke ourselves out, (not in a sexual way), we would just sit along a wall without anything near us and chock ourselves until we passed out. No clue why we thought this was a fun game. I didn't like the game but felt I had to play, so I faked it. I pretended to do it, and then it got scary when one of my friends actually took it seriously. There is no good that comes from this, especially when in the moment of a sexual act it is hard to control it, and what happens if it becomes too late . . .

Here are 10 realizations for some Stepparents:

#1. Do not get into a relationship with someone who has just ended it with the ex of the kids . . . WAIT at least a year because they both need to have moved on.

#2. Wait as long as you can before meeting the kids, this is key for your relationship with their dad. You need a super strong foundation to make this work, as well it gives you time to make sure you actually want the relationship before bringing kids into it. It is not that you don't want to meet the kids, but honestly, once they are in the picture EVERYTHING changes.

#3. Understand that you are NO one's number one, the kids always are first and dad is usually their go to for everything.

#4. Expect that the kids will test you. Constantly. They want to make sure you actually are going to stick through the hard times and not just be another person that leaves them.

#5. Understand, if you do not have your own kids, you may never be called mom. Stepmom all day long but not mom. You might even end up in a relationship where you thought down the road kids would be in your future, but that may never happen.

#6. Once you move in with them, you no longer have your own money. Forget going traveling unless you have a lot of money saved or your total income coming into the house is a lot more than your bills and necessities. You will have weird guilt about spending money on yourself, spending time on yourself or even making the effort to look good every day. I am not going to lie, since living with kids my appearance has absolutely decreased about 50% just because I can't seem to make any more time in the day. Also, working from home gives me zero desire to get out of lululemons for only my dogs to see me.

#7. Your actions, words, values, likes and dislikes can be noticed by the kids. If you drink wine every night, they will call you out on it, and in the back of your mind you want to shout, "Because of you I drink wine." But you can't.

#8. Forget time management. Kids make sure that goes out the window and they RARELY appreciate what you do in the day for them. This might be for anyone with kids but I honestly think that stepkids have less respect for your time.

#9. Don't expect much to come out of Mother's Day. They apparently have a holiday for stepmoms but no one really knows about it since apparently we are not the same as moms.

#10. I do not know if there is a point where you feel like you are truly apart of a family. It is pretty lonely feeling on the outside because you literally are coming in to their lives, you are having to form to their lives, and you pretty much take a back seat.

Be a Turtle

Being a stepmom you really need to get thick skin on, and boy is that hard. You have to be able to tell people why you are in this relationship, even though it shouldn't be their business. You have schools and legal forms telling you that you technically have no rights to anything with the kids, until it is registered in the courts that you are a legal guardian. Your way of parenting a child might not be the way your partner has been/is used to disciplining and his way will trump yours because they aren't your kids.

You are probably thinking, *Whoa, is it really worth it?* It seems like a lot of cons. It takes a special type of person to be able to truly handle and manage a step-relationship. Some days are much easier than others, and some days you just question what the hell you are doing. From what I gather, this isn't just stepmoms, it is parents in general. Our jobs are to help kids not be such assholes, and later in life, you hope for the day where they say they are sorry for everything they put you through.

I know after getting into this relationship I have apologized numerous times to my family about the behaviour they had to deal with when I was younger. It is weird circle of life. You have the kids to grow the generation and hope they take care of you when you are older and they apologize for being an asshole after their kids treat them like an asshole.

But I will tell you that one of the best feelings is when they tell you that they appreciate you being there for them, that you listen, that you don't judge them. I am in a bit of a different situation than most, where I came into a young girl's life after some really tough times since birth. Her mother abandoned her for drugs while her mental health is a struggle, she is living on the streets trying to survive. Most women in her life have not believed anything she has said, or don't understand she is not a boy like the other siblings she grew up with.

There is nothing in your lifetime that can prepare for a crazy journey with a broken family with kids from different parents who really just need someone to love them. I am super hands on because I want to make sure that they feel loved and cared about. My step-daughter made me feel like the best person in the world when she came home one day and said that at school they had to pick someone that they admire in their life and explain why, and of all the people, she picked me. She is not one to voice her feelings about me or how she feels about anything, so seeing she did this project on me was heart melting. I know that what I'm doing is making a difference.

Real Truth . . .

We can all look at Instagram or Facebook or wherever the newest social media trend is to see what everyone else's lives look like to the outside world. You can scroll and scroll and scroll until your self-esteem is beyond low. It makes it seem like everyone else has the perfect life and no issues, or so that is what it is made to look like. Not many people like to talk about the negative things or what is hard about life, because who wants to listen to people bitch? It is either seen as needy attention seekers or just someone who has a really bad day and needs some support. No one wants to talk about the hard stuff, it's too . . . well, hard.

We look for ways to distract ourselves from the bad things in life because it isn't the worst it could be. But here is the truth: Instagram stories show the good things. They do not show everything. Everyone has bad things happen to them.

Raw Truth

I am going to tell you about some real truth here, the kinds of things we can't talk about because no one would understand. As a step-parent, you kind of get mashed into a person who doesn't have the same parenting powers as the co-parent, someone who is expected to just accept how things are, with someone who is required to be more involved with them so the kids feel loved. This mashup has given me so many mindfucks that I couldn't even begin to explain to someone. The best way I can try to explain it is, if you have a triangle trying to go through a square and ends up inside the shape cube and then decides it doesn't make sense so they go out of the cube by a circle. No sense, right?

In a stepparenting role, no situation is the same. Not one broken family situation is the same. No one child is the same. This is the loneliest feeling in the world. Because you have no idea what the fuck you are doing, and no one can give you advice. I have learned that my opinion is lowest on the totem pole; my needs and wants are also down there as well. Just when you think you are doing something right, you are basically told you aren't.

I have spent many moments in tears because I am either too sensitive, too tired, too hungry, too annoyed, or just on empty and still trying to get through, and then all of a sudden the tears come rolling down and that wet trail of pain keeps flowing until finally you just don't have any thing left but to wipe your face, blow your nose, and get into robot mode to get through the day so you can rest your head and hope tomorrow is a better day.

With blended families, I have found there is no one day that is fantastic without something bad happening. We have not gone a day where something has not happened that affected us in some way. And I am not talking about it raining or anything silly like that. It is either a fight with the kids, a fight with the other side, a fight with each other, bills, bad news, emails, or letters. It has been a very long time since I can say that we have had a problem free day.

Here are some lessons that I have learned while being a step mom:

#1. *Be Unapologetic* – this one still to this day is super hard for me. Being myself completely and not apologizing for things, is one of the hardest things I have tried to change about myself. I apologize for everything; if someone makes my food wrong, I don't complain, I just deal with it, or if I do have to then I say I am sorry but . . . Why am I apologizing for someone else's mistake? It is so silly but maybe it is being Canadian that we apologize for everything! I found this really great quote online when I was scrolling on Pinterest one day:

> *Unapologetic – whatever you accept about yourself cannot be used against you. Be willing to own your truth, even if it makes others uncomfortable. The good and the ugly are all part of your story. You never know who you can inspire by being your authentic, unapologetic self.* –Ash Alves

#2. *Find your Voice* – learn to speak up. Say how you feel, say what you need, and for God's sakes, know that your voice actually is important and you aren't just the person who nags everyone. Don't give up your voice, don't give up on your values or your morals. I found this great Instagram account that has a digital magazine and has really great tips and conversations. The account is *@StepMom_Magazine*. It has been a great resource for me and has given me perspective on a lot of things.

#3. *Don't take it personally* – this one is by far a really hard one for me. I take most things said to me personally. I blame myself for the way people feel, what they do or how they act. Which, really, how can I control all of that? I can't control how other people act or what they do. I can only control the things that I actually have control over. I usually blame myself if someone is upset. I push my feelings aside for them. There is a secret though. Most of the time, I am so far wrong, that the person is mad about something else, I just take it as it is my fault. I am just an easier vessel to get mad at because I accept it. My suggestion is to pick your battles. Sometimes you have to bite your tongue so that your sanity is actually intact, and really is it worth fighting with someone who will never be on your side? Children have their own mind and their own feelings of what is right or wrong. You usually are the punching bag but not actually the problem.

#4. *No one is going to understand the situation you are in* – I have said this before and I will say it again, no one blended family is like any other blended family. Your friends without kids will have zero clue what you are going through and the ones with kids can get it for the most part but that emotional/mental piece is harder to understand when they are not biologically your kids. Don't waste your breath telling people your issues, you will have to tell the whole story every time and then you forget what people know and don't know. Pick one or two people who you can go to that understand that they are part of your sanity and community. Without them, you can't survive. It is like when the cavemen use to roam around the planet; if one person went out hunting on their own they may not have come back with much for the tribe, but if multiple people help, then you achieve more. No one person can do a life with kids on their own, let alone a blended family.

#5. *You will probably get compared to the other mom in their life* – I struggle with this one. I feel like I have done nothing but be there for my stepkids and show them how much I care about them. I plan things for them and think about them when I get food and such. When my stepdaughter didn't live with us full time, she would always tell me how much she hated going to the other house. She said she was always cleaning up after everyone, that she was forced to eat food she didn't like, that it was gluten free everything and it was not good to eat. She told me she was left out of everything and very alone. Throw in the alcoholism of this woman and lack of taking care of the kids—we got her out of this situation. It has NOT been easy, nor an enjoyable time.

It is always something, with no break from the attitude anymore. Today she told me she misses the other house because they would do fun things because of the younger kid and not once has she ever told me that she enjoys those things, let alone says thank you when I do something nice for her. It is beyond frustrating to be compared to someone who clearly has her own demons.

I think kids don't understand that we as adults have feelings too. It is never an easy battle with kids, and it is worse with kids who have been through so much. You really have to learn quick how to put up your turtle shell and let things slide off your back. It isn't easy, let me tell you.

#6. *Find your Community* – This is no joke here, parenting, you can't do it alone. Finding the people you can vent to, ask advice, listen to their stories, and grow together as a team is one of the most important things. I have been through so much as a stepparent, and if I didn't reach out to my community I would be lost. Also, the community should keep growing, find people who can help you with things. I have had to build relationships with my kid's teachers, school counselors, principals, etc. Each person is in your life for either a season, a reason, or a lifetime.

The one thing I have learned that was a huge eye opener was from the school counselor at my stepdaughter's school. She told me that she read a book about parenting, and throughout the book, the theme was that you have to figure out yourself before you can figure out your kids. You need to focus on finding what your triggers are, your raw emotions from your past that can be triggered by situations with your kids. If you don't know your triggers, it can get really hard for kids to understand.

Great example: when the kids talk about their moms, I feel like I am being compared to them. That I am doing something wrong, or they like them more than me. I put all of the blame on myself. When in actual fact, they are just telling me about things that go on when I am not around. My trigger is: when I was younger I would be compared and blamed for things.

So I have to understand that when I get upset or angry, it is not that the child is doing it to me, they could be joking, but I take it to be hurtful because that's what I'm used to. Someone talks about someone else, instantly I am the one under the microscope, when in actual fact, it is just in my head that I feel this way.

Stepparenting is extremely difficult, and I give huge props to anyone that does it. If you are considering being a stepparent, please listen to my advice and make sure you are in it for the long haul.

"The biggest regret any stepmom can have is to lose years of herself by shape shifting to please and care for her stepfamily. You're a person first and foremost, not simply someone who fills a role in a household."

—StepMom Magazine

CHAPTER 6

THE UNICORN GREW HER HORN

✳ Trigger Warning – Topic about Self Harm/Suicide ✳

"Teenager (noun): When you're too young for half the things you want to do and too old to do the other half."

—Unknown

Here is the way I see young girls: they are young cute fillies that are awkward and just follow the beat of their own drums. Once the young girl is a pre-teen, she has become a horse. When the pre-teen turns into a full blown teenager that is when the horse grows a horn to become the mystical unicorn. A unicorn is one of those creatures that everyone wishes they could have. A teenager, on the other hand . . .

I compare these two creatures because they are both unknown. You never know what you are going to get with a teenager, which hormonal creature will come out. Every girl wants to be a unicorn, wants to be accepted, wants everyone to want to be around them.

But in reality, girls are mean; they don't want to uplift anyone. They tend to put others down because they are so confused in their lives they don't even know what to expect or what they truly want. Mystical creatures are hard to figure out and make sense of, just like teenagers—75% of the time, they don't make any sense and that can be confusing and hard. For everyone involved. Heck, they don't even know what they want or need half of the time themselves!

I also use this creature as a comparison because once those girls turn into teenagers their hormones are through the roof; they don't know what feelings they are feeling or what they even mean. One of the biggest things that is confusing for females is who they are interested in for a partner. Sometimes it can be the same sex or the opposite. It is more accepted in the world today to be a same sex couple, or bi-sexual, or to believe you are in the wrong body.

I will tell you when my stepdaughter turned fourteen, everything went to an extreme. All she seems to want to think about or talk about is sex and things that relate to it. I believe that open communication is super important in this situation. Not judging, not jumping to anger, but actually listening and answering questions. If she doesn't come to you, then your friend Google might be used a little more than it should. I believe being open and honest with your child is key. You need to make them feel like no matter what they can come to you.

When I was younger, I did not feel like I had this support. I was scared that no matter what I said I would get in trouble or be a disappointment. Especially when it came to my choice of boyfriends. I also felt like, with everything going on, that I would just be more of a disappointment to my family because I blamed my self. I put myself in the situations and I didn't do anything to help myself. I wish I'd had someone to talk to and tell, but I felt so alone it didn't help. I felt I had to measure up to my sister and still to this day this is something I battle.

Social Media

Now, with this generation of teenagers, it is all about social media and the likes and comments. I can tell when my stepdaughter has been on her phone nonstop because of the attitude she comes with, her hiding in her room and not wanting to even acknowledge that we exist. We call this stage "screen-itude." When she has her phone taken away she is more happy, present, and talkative. I strongly believe that social media for teens can cause such anxiety, bullying, mental health issues, and confidence destroying issues. They constantly have to be holding their phone to make sure they don't miss anything. It is also easy for people to say things without any consequences. My girl had a boy tell her he was going to make her watch him kill himself. THIS IS NOT OKAY.

I also strongly believe that teenagers should not be on phones after ten p.m. After that, who knows what happens on there; from what I have witnessed, it is not good. They go on live videos and asks random people to dare them to do things, or they talk to random people all over the world. They take naked pictures and send them to the people they like. Which, by the way, is child pornography and is illegal! And if you think your child has not done this, you need to check their phones. I have walked in on her naked on FaceTime while the boy masturbates, while telling her to do things to herself. Worst part? She didn't even like him! She just did it for attention.

And for those kids who think it is not a big deal, tell them that once it is on the Internet, ANYONE can see it and then masturbate while looking at their picture. If you need to get the photo back from the person they sent it to, talk to the police and they will get it wiped from the phone. It can also affect them in the future with potential jobs or situations that if people found those photos they could be in a lot of trouble. Now a days employers use social media to look into people they are interviewing… nothing is completely removed from the internet, so things from childhood can catch up to you!

Influencers?

People get famous on TikTok for making up a dance or "sound" and it goes viral and people copy what you do and post it. The current top TikTok persons is Charli D'Amelio. She is sixteen years old and has over eighty-four million followers. For what I call flailing of arms and shaking your body. I don't really know how people can call this a "job." Some people can make a ton of money doing things on here, but you also have to have a thick skin so you are not upset over the haters. There are always haters.

When you ask kids what they want to be when they grow up, I am hearing the word "influencer" come up—Youtubers, TikTokers, etc. It scares me to think that kids want to do this as a job because we are going to miss out on a huge generation of jobs that are needed to be filled. Currently there are more seniors than children, and once the baby boomers are no longer around, we are left to hope that the younger generations will take over their jobs. We need to help kids think about actual occupations again. Nothing against influencers on social media, but something can happen and they lose all their followers and then have NOTHING to fall back on. Think about that . . .

Self-Harm

Self-harm is another topic we need to talk about with our kids, teens, adults sometimes too. Self-harm is not something to joke about or threaten for attention. Nine times out of ten they are just saying it to have someone stop them . . . it is the people who don't talk about it that actually will go through with it, or try to. I know the series *13 Reasons Why* on Netflix got a bad rap for talking about everything it did, but to be honest I think it is a key show to watch with parents and teens. They should sit down and watch it and talk about what happens together. The things talked about in this show are everyday issues that, most of the time, we do not hear about. I also think that people only see it from the girl's perspective, when actually if you think about how she felt, with the parents who were too busy in their lives to realize she was showing signs of needing help, maybe she wouldn't have committed suicide.

Signs and symptoms of self-injury may include:

- Scars, often in patterns
- Fresh cuts, scratches, bruises, bite marks or other wounds
- Excessive rubbing of an area to create a burn
- Keeping sharp objects on hand
- Wearing long sleeves or long pants, even in hot weather
- Frequent reports of accidental injury
- Difficulties in interpersonal relationships
- Behavioral and emotional instability, impulsivity and unpredictability
- Statements of helplessness, hopelessness or worthlessness
- Forms of self-injury
- Self-injury usually occurs in private and is done in a controlled or ritualistic manner that often leaves a pattern on the skin. Examples of self-harm include:
    - Cutting (cuts or severe scratches with a sharp object)
    - Scratching
    - Burning (with lit matches, cigarettes or heated, sharp objects such as knives)
    - Carving words or symbols on the skin
    - Self-hitting, punching or head banging
    - Piercing the skin with sharp objects
    - Inserting objects under the skin
    - Most frequently, the arms, legs and front of the torso are the targets of self-injury, but any area of the body may be used for self-injury. People who self-injure may use more than one method to harm themselves. (*Mayo Clinic. n.d.*)

Suicide Should NOT be Threatened to Get Attention

Kids these days seem to use suicide threats as an attention thing. My stepdaughter told me about this friend she has, that told her he wants to hurt himself and it is all he thinks about. Once day he told her that he tried to slit his wrists and throat and was in the hospital basically on suicide watch. She saw him a couple days later and he had no marks on him whatsoever—so she felt confused why he would say that if it was not true.

I have had a few suicide scares with my stepdaughter as well. The first one happened when she was at school. She texted me saying she was sorry and was scared. She took some liquid Tylenol and she needed help. I was freaking out and called her principal, and he found her but she was in class laughing . . . not hiding in a bathroom, scared, like she told me. I took her to the hospital as I was taking it seriously but as well when they declare they are suicidal at school, they are required to send her to the hospital with a parent, and she made it into a game. She was all fine while we waited and then she told the counselor she was thinking about it but promised not to hurt herself. We got home and she was laughing and all fine. So I thought maybe it was her way of trying to move past it.

Then recently she was in trouble and told her grandma that she was thinking about harming herself with pills again. So I got told by the grandma, and I was on the phone with the crisis line, collecting all of the pills around the house, and she came home from school like nothing had happened and made food and watched a show. I spent four hours trying to figure out why she was behaving like this, and she manipulated me fully! Gave me a sob story about how hard her life is and shit—but she is not helping the situation. She hates getting in trouble but does things that she knows will get her in trouble, like stealing or lying.

To top it off, we called her doctor to talk about her thoughts and she told the doctor she was cutting herself for self-harm and to feel something other than sadness. I asked her after the call to show me her legs where she was cutting, so I could make sure that they were not infected. She was instantly worried. She told me no she didn't want to show me. I told her she had to and the actual story came out, that she'd only nicked herself a couple times while shaving but there were no scars or anything. She'd made it seem so much worse, and I just don't understand how she can lie like that.

It actually hurts me a lot to go through this with her, because I had my own suicidal thoughts, and one time was going to go through with it. I was tired of being abused and bullied by my boyfriend at the time; my family wanted nothing to do with me because I basically pushed them away whenever they were saying things about my relationship. I thought I was in love, that I had it all with this relationship which was actually one of the absolute shittiest relationships of my life. Every time I hear about a teenager wanting to hurt themselves I think back to the one night that I will never forget. I do not remember the reason why or how we even were in the situation we were, but the moment of the decision is what is stuck in my head.

In Chapter 2, when I spoke about my run-ins with self-harm, those are things I never told anyone except for one time. I wanted to do it, but what stopped me was thinking about my family and how it would affect them. Again, I am a person who thinks about others before myself and I believe in this case it saved me. Whereas most people who want to harm themselves don't think about what happens after they are gone, who it affects and how it can affects people that care about them. Sometimes we need to take a moment in the day and make sure we are noticing how people are in our lives. There are always signs someone is hurting and needs some help. Most people will not ask for help or want to be a burden. It is important to ask people, "Are you really okay?"

Kids are Always Listening

As I was growing up it was instilled into my brain that women should look a certain way, and if they aren't that way, then they are not beautiful. I can tell you I looked more than once at photos and thought, *I will never be that small or pretty*. Add that to the mental abuse of getting told by my boyfriends that I was ugly and fat and that no one would want me.

Please read that again.

I let people talk to me like that, I let people get into my head and tell me that I am not pretty or the right look for them. To comment on a female's weight is just not helpful in any way. Don't talk to you child about their body except to teach them how it works. Don't say anything if they have lost or gained weight. If you really think you need to comment then try things like, "You are looking so healthy," or, "You are looking really strong." Or better yet, don't say anything at all about their body, say something that has nothing to do with how their body looks. Sometimes bringing attention to things can upset them or make them stress about it.

Don't ever talk about YOUR hate for your body in front of your child. Don't talk about any diets you are on, as it gives them the idea that you need to diet. Just eat healthy and explain to them the importance of why. Don't talk about carbs as though they are the enemy. Shaming yourself about what you eat is just going to cause you to feel bad and then the kids see it too. But you can have open communication around food and how some help you and some does not. I think kids just see the yummy junk food and not necessarily what it is doing to their body.

I can tell you that when I was a teen I ate whatever the hell I wanted. My go-to was banana milkshakes and pasta with butter and parmesan. Not the best diet, let me tell you, but I was happy because I enjoyed it. However, once I hit twenty my body no longer allowed me to eat what I wanted, and my weight exploded.

Do Encourage Kids

DO encourage your children to learn about kindness towards others. How females can also do "men's jobs." The important of independence and learning how to take care of yourself. Encourage them to stick to the sport or hobby they love. Encourage them to figure out what makes them feel good in life. Help them find love for things in life. Without love, we inflict hate on ourselves because we know we should be doing something else. Keeping busy and having the confidence that you can crush the new hobby makes you have less time to hate anything about yourself. Also, let them know they might not be good at it all to start, but don't give up when it's hard. Don't give up.

Teach your children how to admit when they are wrong, explain the meaning of "I am sorry" and crying wolf, push them out of their comfort zone, make them learn to talk about their emotions and be okay to feel all of the feelings. Be that strong light in their life so they have something to strive towards. Be that positive aspect in their life, but also know it is okay to have bad days too. Show them how to get out of the bad day and move on. Teach them how to cook their favourite meal, or bake their favourite cake. Explain to them that likes on social media do not mean they have that many friends. Show them how to use their imagination. Always tell them you love them before they go to sleep. And most importantly, never give up on them.

Don't Speak of Adult Things Around Them

Don't talk about big scary things in front of your kids, especially at a young age. We currently rent the place we are in and have had some issues with neighbours and the property management company. We received a letter basically stating the next one will be an eviction notice and my partner and I were so upset. We were talking about it around the kids and a couple weeks later I found my stepson in his room crying. He said he was worried we would have nowhere to live if we got kicked out, and that he doesn't want to leave his friends. So this fully affected him and I had no idea until much later. Broke my heart. Kids are ALWAYS listening and when you talk about big things around them, it can truly affect them and you may have no idea.

*"It's rough being a teenager
in this day and age."*

–Kay Panabaker

CHAPTER 7

SELF CARE

*"Fall in love with the process of becoming
the very best version of yourself."*

—Unknown

I know that everyone preaches about self care. "What have you done for self care? What way do you keep your stress down?" I was always one of those people who was like, "I just don't have time." I don't even know how to put myself first. I actually was at the point where I thought I had to ask my family for permission to have a bath. Just to make sure everyone else was taken care of before I did something for myself.

For people such as myself, it is really hard to put yourself first over everyone else. I personally have a super hard time with this, but I've realized that a car can't drive without gas, and if it's on empty it is good for no one. That is the same as your body. You can't continue at the rate you are going if you never take a break. You must fill up your gas tank or your cup! I am not saying take days off from life, but take an hour a day to do something that fills up your cup. We want to see cups full, not empty.

In case you were not aware, there are actually six different kinds of self care categories:

1. **Physical Self Care** – *Involves activities that improve your physical health, such as diet and exercise.*

   This category is what I would think most people would consider as self care. The recommendation to move your body, get the blood flowing, heart pumping, getting that alive feeling is key to help fill up your cup of life. It can help with bad moods, anxiety, stress levels, sore bodies, and an overall distraction from the world. Make sure whatever you pick to spend time doing, that you actually enjoy it. It is important. Otherwise it is just another thing you should be doing that you dread getting up to do; it should never feel like an obligation.

   Some ideas:
   - Yoga
   - Hiking or walking in nature
   - Bike ride
   - Eat more veggies and fruit
   - Drink more water throughout the day

2. **Emotional Self Care** – *is caring for your emotional needs by identifying what it is your feeling and then moving forward in a way that honours yourself and those emotions.*

   A lot of people find this hard, spending time in quiet with your thoughts and feelings is not everyone's favourite past time. Trying to understand why you feel the way you do and how to overcome it before overwhelming feelings start to take over.

   Some ideas:
   - Daily journaling to put your feelings and emotions down on paper

- Change the negative self talk to being more positive
- Express your emotions through creativity
- Understand when you need to say no and set realistic boundaries
- Know when you need a break to just be by yourself, and know that is okay!

3. **Spiritual Self Care** – *is the activity we engage in to find and nurture a sense of connection to a Higher Power and meaning for our lives.*

I believe that most people only see spiritual care as praying, or going to church. But it is actually whatever YOU want to believe in. It can be religion, it can be tarot cards or psychics, etc. Whatever you feel comfortable believing it and spending time learning about is what you should do under this category. Don't force it, don't feel pressured to join a religion unless you want to. Remember this is to help YOU, no one else.

Some ideas:
- Practice daily meditation
- Spend time in nature
- Volunteer for a cause you believe in
- Learn about a form of spiritually you are interested in

4. **Intellectual Self Care** – *addresses your inner "thinker" and by cultivating a healthy intellect you can expand your knowledge and mindset. It's an important step to take when keeping all aspects of yourself in the best condition because a healthy mind is the foundation of a healthy self.*

This category is sometimes overlooked by people. We are constantly doing and learning things on the daily, so it seems weird to actually focus on this category when you are most likely doing some of the things on the list below. Here is the kicker, because this seems not as important as, say, physical self care because maybe you "don't have the time" or think that sitting down to read a book is selfish. Stop it. Stop thinking like this. To read a book for thirty minutes is more relaxing than doing those dishes that can wait. Just remember it does not have to be an all day thing, just spend thirty minutes a day; you will find you are more relaxed and potentially smarter!

Some ideas:
- Read a book
- Take a course/class
- Learn a new hobby
- Watch a documentary on a topic you know nothing about

5. **Social Self Care** – *involves just having fun with the people you love. It means talking effectively through conflict, and addressing the emotional needs of the people you love.*

This one might be the easiest for people who are extroverts or just enjoy being around people. Take this one with a balance. I am not saying spend all your time around people, have the balance of alone time and time with others, but make it about having fun.

Some ideas:
- Reconnect with an old friend
- Plan a girls night
- Be around people you love

6. **Sensory Self Care** – *is all about helping to calm your mind; when you are able to tune into the details of the sensations all around you, it's easier to live in the present moment. When you think about practicing sensory self care, consider all of your senses: touch, smell, sound, and sight.*

This one is the newest for me, I never thought about exciting the senses as self care. I can't say I focus on this category much except for taking baths, because I find it is the best time to relax, read, have my good smelling bath bombs, and melt into the hot water where all your stress disappears out of your body, down the drain. I never thought about enjoying the smell of homemade cookies or dinner being made as self care, but after being in the moment and seeing how it makes me feel— paying attention to my body—I instantly take a deep breath in, smell the goodness, and smile. So I guess it does work! Give it a try—who doesn't love smelling homemade cookies? Try to do it without smiling, I dare you!

Some ideas:
- Write in a gratitude journal
- Burn your favourite smelling candle
- Bake your favourite kind of cookies
- Take a warm bath with Epsom salts, bath bomb and bubble bath
- Have a dance party to your favourite music

In the end, the result is your feeling of being balanced and calm. Can you imagine having a really long day full of doing things for other people and you carve out one hour a day to do something for you? If I don't get time, even thirty minutes, to do something that fills up my cup in a day, let's just say I am not very pleasant to be around.

Don't you love when you stumble across something that leads to something amazing? Let's be honest, we probably miss a lot of amazing things around us just being "too busy" in life. Not spending the time to notice these things can be a huge happiness loss. So my win was actually on Instagram. I had an amazing creative friend who was part of a giveaway. You had to follow everyone who was involved in the giveaway. So I followed all of the makers and then kept coming across this one account that caught my eye. She was a lovely maker who does CBD bath bombs, bath salts, etc. I finally realized I needed a really good bath with an amazing bath bomb. I was looking at all of the items the maker had, and I was so excited to pick a couple options.

I came across this really amazing "Self Love Box" and here is what was inside:

- 1 Handpicked Self Love Affirmation Card
- 1 Self Love Bliss Bomb
- 2 Tubes of our Salt Soak
- 1 Candle
- 1 Stick of Palo Santo
- 1 Selenite crystal
- 1 Rose Quartz crystal
- 1 Amethyst crystal
- 1 Black Onyx crystal
- 1 Self Love Lip Balm
- And zero reasons for you to put off loving yourself any further

I read this whole list a couple times a day and I kept coming back to the last thing she said . . . zero reasons for you to put off loving yourself any further. Well DAMN! So I did it, I ordered this amazing box of goodies, plus a few extra bath bombs, because why not?

The box arrived super quickly and I waited until the end of the week to have a nice quiet bath after my stepson went to his mom's house. It was a long, long week with this COVID-19 pandemic. I was exhausted and trying to keep the stress down and decided to do this lovely self love box. I was also doing a lot of negative talk, so we needed to fix that. I got everything set up for this bath and here is the ritual that I did:

- Ran the bath with my pink Himalaya mineral bath soak.
- I set up the bath with my unwrapped bath bomb, laid out the crystals, lit my candle, and had my affirmation card laying out as well.
- I removed all of my clothes.
- I took the stick of Palo Santo and lit it with the candle. Once it started smoking I closed my eyes and stood in tree pose.
- Moved my hand with the Palo Santo stick all over the bath, around the room as well up and down my body, front and back.

- As I was moving the smoke around, I said nice things to myself. I told myself that I loved myself, that I am beautiful, that I am amazing and strong. I also asked to bless the room from any negativity to move forward.
- I climbed in to the bath, dropped my amazing bath bomb into the bath; I took the crystals in both my hands, closed my eyes and took three deep breathes.
- Opened up my eyes and looked at the affirmation card that was picked for me in the box. I read what the note was while holding the crystals in my hands. I flipped the card over and read the other side. Took a deep breath and then read them in the reverse order. Once I was done, I took the crystals and put one on the right side of my body, the left side, the front of the bath and then one behind me and then said, "I love you."
- I slowly sank into the bath and I instantly felt like I was being hugged. It was a pretty weird feeling, but then I relaxed into it and it was like someone was hugging me, no joke! I've never felt more relaxed and calm after a bath. This was by far the best bath I have had. I got out feeling revived, recharged, relaxed, and with super soft skin.

This was a magical thing that I did for myself, and I hope you can find something just as good!

The other thing I want to say is that self care can be overwhelming, but just know that simply doing nothing is self care. Sitting on the couch with a coffee or glass of wine and staring at the wall or watching your favourite Netflix show, and you are doing nothing. That can be your care. If everything else feels impossible right now, then start with this. Because starting is the first step. You will see a difference in yourself once you start doing self care, and your body will crave it and make sure to tell you when it's time if it has been too long. Listen to your body.

Be gentle with yourself.

"Your greatest responsibility is to love yourself and to know you are enough."

–Unknown

CHAPTER 8

MY TWO CENTS FOR ALL IT'S WORTH

"Be strong, but not rude; Be kind, but not weak; Be bold, but not bully; Be humble, but not timid; Be proud, but not arrogant."

—Unknown

Children . . .

For those of you with kids or thinking about having kids . . . my best advice would be to try to have the relationship with them where they can talk to you about anything without you getting upset with them. Growing up, I never felt like I had someone "safe" to talk to, where I wouldn't get grounded or in trouble. Not saying that you shouldn't punish them, but pick your battles. I have had conversations with my stepdaughter that I never would have had with my parents. Granted, she says she can't talk to her dad because he will just get mad. There are some things I really want to get mad at her for, but I know if I do, I will lose that trust and open conversation instantly.

Another point is that they are listening, whether you think they are or not. For the longest time I thought I was just talking to talk and she wasn't listening to me but then I found out later that she actually does listen, she just doesn't want me to know she appreciates my advice. Because it is exactly that, advice. Not telling her what to do, or telling her what I would do, giving her the advice/tools and letting her deal with it is key. Sometimes she picks and chooses what information she listens to, which sometimes is not what I actually meant, but when she makes a choice that she would have made the opposite one if I didn't say anything, then I have to take that as a win. I also have sometimes had to share some of my stories with her so she understands the ramifications of some of her actions and that I understood how she was feeling.

I have been reading a lot of books on parenting and the one thing that I have learned is that if you tell them NOT to do something, they are going to do it. Teenagers can't wait for freedom and to make their own decisions. As an adult, our job is not to make the decisions and shield them from the life choices, but to teach them how to grow and be independent to make those decisions. It is ultimately then their consequences to deal with, they cannot blame you for them, as you did not make the choice. You provide them with advice and let them do what they are going to do. Because, regardless, as I said before, if you tell them no, they will do it. So let them, to an extent.

Trust me that is a hard lesson to learn as a parent, because all you want to do is protect them from the bad things in life, but once they are on their own, no one but them can protect themselves. I find that, for myself, I am grateful that I am independent because I know how to do a lot more things, or know where to go to find answers, over someone who has been bubble wrapped their whole childhood.

I just wish there were not so many bad things that can happen. Kids don't know how to deal with things, or they fall for peer pressure—which, if you have to be pressured to do something, it is probably not the best idea.

Health...

So in Canada we have it pretty good; going to the doctor is free for the most part. We have benefits to cover alternative health measures, as well as prescriptions. This is all great. However, this means that the lineups at the walk-in clinics are hours waiting; people come in for the smallest things to be sent home with a bed rest prescription.

The biggest issue is also the fact that to find a family doctor that you can call your own is nearly impossible. So sometimes we need to take things into our own hands to try to figure out what is wrong. I am mostly talking about my situation; I have health issues, but no matter what, when I go to the doctor, or do blood tests, x-rays, ultrasounds, etc., they all come back fine. I am getting the rap sheet that my issues are "in my head." Did you know that is literally the most maddening thing to hear when you are just looking for help to feel less awful, and you are told it is in your head? You tell me, would you be smiling and skipping out of the doctor's office? Normally I walk away and have a good cry in the car. Another disappointing doctor's appointment.

So the next step is to try to figure out what is going on without any help, or at least nontraditional support. Instead of jumping on Google and looking up your symptoms—because let's be honest here, you have already done this multiple times, let's not waste any more time on that. I am a big believer in physical books being in my hands while I read them. I like feeling the weight of them, seeing how far I have got through the book, holding it in my hands, etc. I am on a screen all day with work and I just really enjoy holding a good book. What I have been working on is finding books that I can order online about different things that can help me.

If the doctor says it is in my head then let's look at how to control stress, have more spiritual presence in my life, look at what I am eating and how I can change that. No one is going to fight for answers except ourselves. Don't waste time waiting for the answer to hit you in the face, start taking your own health into your hands. It is going to take time and money, but you only have one body, and isn't it worth fighting for?

Money...

This is such a sensitive topic, but I wish I would have had someone talk to me about money and what it actually means, when I was a teenager. We just think that money grows on trees at this age. Then we get older and we have a job and work, spend money, obviously not saving anything for when you are older. Get approved for your first credit card—woohoo, free money! Wait, no one told you that you have to pay it back and you get charged interest? Whoops...

If you can learn one thing from this: budget. Learn how to budget, learn what a budget means and what it can do for you. I got a really awesome book for budgeting because it makes you track every day what you spend and where it all goes. It is a book called *Sort Your $hit Out: A Monthly Budget Planner by Jackson A David.* It starts with a budget page for the month, what you are anticipating. Then it asks you to fill in each day what you spend, add it up each week and at the end you have a total of what you spent and where and how off you were on your budget for the month compared to your income. I have never been one to follow through with this, but I am on month four and I am loving it. It is so helpful to see where we are spending most of the money.

Travel...

Just. Do. It.

Travel as much and as often as you possibly can. It is the only thing money can buy that you will never regret.

I have a map of the world on my wall, and I put stickers on it when I travel somewhere new. So much is left in the world I have not touched and once this pandemic lets up, I will be back on the travel train!

Growing up, my parents took us to places like Disneyland, Hawaii, and mainly the USA. The first time I travelled by myself and off the North American Continent was when I was in my early twenties and I was in a rut. I had hired a life coach and she convinced me to just do it. Book a trip and do it. So I did, I picked a fifty-day Contiki camping trip around Europe. Boy, was this an adventure and something I had no concept of. This was a life changing experience and I am glad I did it. We travelled around Europe on a bus and stayed in cabins or tents. I went to twenty-four different cities, and I cannot wait to go back again to Europe! Highly recommend traveling once you are done high school; book a group trip like Contiki, where you can meet people from all over the world!

I made some lifelong bonds on this trip and have since visited a couple of friends who live in New Zealand and Australia—and the best part was, I had somewhere to stay and didn't have to pay for a hotel. Some of the best times of my life! Almost ten years later, and I still have memories that are triggered by songs, words, places, etc. And these memories are good ones that are triggered! Don't waste your time on this Earth by staying in the same place.

Just. Go. #noregrets!

Love...

Ahh this is a tricky one . . . it is what we all want. Regardless of whether or not someone says they want love, they do. Every human requires the void to be filled. I feel like until social media became a huge thing in everyone's lives, growing up as a little girl I thought to myself how I needed to find the perfect husband, perfect kids and perfect little house with the perfect job.

One thing that has stuck out in my past relationships is that I pick people who are not on my level; they need some support to fix something or just need someone to be devoted to them. I have officially learned that if you do not love yourself, or you don't see great things for yourself, no one else is going to see that. If you do not love yourself, how can you expect someone else to love you?

It is okay to take yourself on a date, it is okay to tell yourself every day you love yourself. It is highly recommended to have a strong foundation as to what you want in a relationship or what expectations you have. What are your hard limits and boundaries that, no matter what, you will stick to? I never really followed this, I just went with whoever gave me attention. IF you can learn anything at all from this book, it is please don't do this. Please don't put everyone's needs in front of yours. You are just as important as everyone else, if not more. You should have YOU as your number one.

Listen to your body, it can tell you amazing things. I learned that stress is a HUGE contributor to my weight gain, unhappiness, etc. I see how stress affects me physically, emotionally, and mentally. Take your power back and live in love for yourself, and NEVER give up your power to do what feels good for you.

Love yourself first, always.

"Never give up on what you really want to do. The person with big dreams is more powerful than one with all the facts."

—Albert Einstein

CHAPTER 9

THE RAW TRUTH

"When you show up authentic, you create the space for others to do the same. Walk in your Truth."

—Unknown

After picking up this self-help book, thinking, *Oh, I really hope I get something out of this book*, you must be wondering, *What is her life like now?* Well, great question. I actually was struggling with how to share this, I almost didn't even put it in the book . . . because I was ashamed.

I had to talk to a friend about how I could put this in the book. How could I be that raw and open to the judging and criticism that I might get for this?

My friend said, "If what you are about to share is the truth, and in this case it's important to be truthful, then it can be painted any which way you choose. It's never a joke, just honesty. Continue to write honestly; if you don't, it invalidates the intent and the progress you've made thus far."

I literally dropped my jaw . . . if not now, then when? Why be ashamed of my truth? Well, once I give you the download of what is going on currently, you might see why I was ashamed. But I will also share with you the points that my friend told me and how they play a part in my story.

Have you ever been a part of something where you were on the outside? Truly on the outside, where your thoughts, actions, ideas, and wants don't matter? Well when you are with someone who has a child with a trauma background (I am not sure if it applies to all kids or not, but it does in my situation), you will never be number one. You will always be told you are too hard on her, you expect too much. You criticize her too much, she isn't "always perfect." NO MATTER WHAT, this will be the fight.

I can't even count how many times I have been told all of these things. That I just expect way too much of her. This is what I asked from her: pick up after yourself, do your homework, help out once in a while, don't make crazy experiments at midnight. I used to come downstairs in the morning to a massive mess of whatever from an experiment she thought would be good, usually with food. It was such a nightmare to deal with when I first woke up.

I was never asking for too much. The biggest thing was I rarely heard her say "thank you" or "sorry." Yes, maybe I am too sensitive and have the feelings out most of the time, but when you do everything for someone and plan your day around them, make sure they have the best birthday during quarantine, cook and clean for them—a thank you sometimes would be nice. Apparently this is expecting too much.

When you ask the fourteen-year-old, why can't you just say "thank you" or "sorry"? Her response is, "It is awkward." She can't explain why. So I brought it to her dad to talk about why this might be and he would blow up, saying the above things and finish off by saying, "I blame myself because I am her dad and obviously I didn't do something right." Things would get a bit heated, so I'd walk away.

A few moments later, he would come find me and say sorry and explain what he meant. I told him how I took it and he said that was not the case. I explained to him that I was trying to help her think about the future and not just be in the moment, thinking about screens all the time. I am trying to teach her life skills because she has said to me so many times, "Why can't we learn things in school that are actually helpful outside of school."

I am trying to help her learn the things that she clearly has not been exposed to. Responsibility and Respect. The two most important things in order to go anywhere in this world.

It has been a really frustrating cycle I have been in, trying to help everyone else but myself. I lost my soul, my spirit, my drive, and my willingness to succeed in life. My life wrapped around my stepkids and household. I work from home and in summertime the kids are home most of the time. So it is very difficult to separate life and work and dealing with all the crap that has come into my life. I went into a deep depression and I could not get out of it. I ended up getting physically ill and in so much pain; no tests or doctors could tell me what was wrong. The end result: STRESS.

Did you know stress can kill? Stress is something that can come into your life and cause havoc on your body. Sometimes we don't want to believe that stress is not a factor; you can handle anything that life throws at you. I am sorry but I have debunked this myth! If stress gets to be too much and constant, your body is always in fight or flight mode and that is depleting your adrenal glands, which is NOT a good thing.

When I got to my darkest hole and I realized that no one but me can fix the situation, it was time to figure out a new plan. Something HAD to change otherwise the hospital was calling my name. My doctor tried to put me on anti-depression meds and it made me feel so much worse; I had crazy side effects and it was just too much to handle. My body was telling me that I did not need drugs to feel better; it was within me to find. I had to listen to my body and my mind to see what was going on. Once I stopped taking the meds I started feeling so much better as each day when on. I told my doctor that was not an option and I wanted to try to work on things myself.

This was really difficult, to basically depend on myself to figure out a solution. But if no doctors or any medical person could help me, then I had to figure out what was going on. So I started a new journey, one that was for me. It meant that I had to make hard decisions and say no to things. I had to step back as a parent, partner, and household runner. I sat myself down and said, *Okay what are we going to do?*

I put it out to the Universe to help guide me to where I needed to go and what I needed to be focusing on. Things started showing up in my life that I probably would have ignored if I wasn't paying attention. I found some amazing groups, challenges, new friends, and people who were positive. I also took counseling very seriously and used multiple sources of individuals and resources. Even though it was up to me to make changes, I didn't have to do it alone. I just had to be willing to open up my mind and soul to new things. I had to be open and vulnerable.

This happens around us whether we are listening and paying attention or not. Sometimes things come up and we just don't see it. We don't hear it. Unless we open our hearts, minds, eyes, and ears, we will miss it. I can't explain how it feels to be open to opportunities and what I have learned from this. I know that I have so many goals and dreams I have put off because I was so focused on others. Everything has shifted for me and it feels so good. I don't know what the future has in store for me but I am finally seeing some positive things that could be life changing!

Changes I Have Made

In case you were wondering what I have been doing that has been so life changing for me, I will share my secret! I want as many people in the world to find their soul and spirit and live the best life possible so I would be happy to share what I have been doing.

The biggest shift in mindset for me has come from starting a morning routine. I have been hearing for years how a morning routine changes your day and life for the better. I actually thought this was actual crap. I love sleeping WAY too much to get up any earlier than I wanted to. So I tried to find things I could do throughout the day that would be part of a morning routine. The only problem I had was that I couldn't stay focused on it. If I did things all over the place then I never fully completed what I was wanting to and then I felt disappointed I couldn't be consistent with it.

Then it felt so farfetched that I gave up. I said, *There is no way I can do this.* I had a lot of self talk that was negative during this time. I believe it was because I was trying something new and still was in the place of doing everything for everyone else and not focusing on me. I went a few days without touching my list of things and I felt like I was going backwards again. I stopped and took a deep breathe and said, *Okay, what have I done that made me feel good? What have I stopped doing that may of actually helped me?*

Basically it came down to telling myself I need to be consistent and give it the time it needs. I am always trying to get things done quick and move on to the next. Stopping and taking time to listen to myself and my body, felt impossible. Meditation was something I HATED doing because I felt I was doing it wrong. I rarely could quiet my mind for 1 second let alone 10-20 minutes.

Did you know that meditation can't be done wrong? Only you judge yourself on your meditation. No one else is around, and side note, if there is, they probably are not focusing on your practice, they are focusing on their own. So get out of your head, literally, and sit and listen to your mind and body. I find a guided meditation is super helpful because it reminds you to just let the thoughts pass by and to not focus on it or get mad about having a thought pop in. The basic idea of it, is trying to calm or quiet your mind. This is a skill that takes a long time to master and consistency is key. If you only do it once in a while it won't become a habit. It will be something you might actually dread.

My Morning Routine

In case you were curious on what I am doing for my changes and the positive impact it has had on my life, read below for the details!

Night Before . . .

The night before I will check my calendar for what I have going on with work, personal, and the house hold. Once I am aware of everything in the day, I plan what time I need to be up. I like to give myself a minimum of an hour to do my morning routine so it is not rushed. Rushing it defeats the purpose of it! Once I know what time I have to be up I set my alarm and set my intention to NOT snooze this in the morning (some mornings are harder than others). If I do snooze it, then I make sure it is one time, and usually I take that snooze as time to wake up gentler.

I always make sure my items are within grabbing distance so that if I am snuggled up with my pups I don't have to disturb everyone just to get my books. I have been changing up my flow of how I do things and I think I have finally mastered the best way of doing it.

Meditation/Manifestation

The first thing I do is completely ignore any notifications on my phone and I open up my Headspace app. You can get this app for free and use the options in there; I am not sure if what I am doing is part of the free version but I highly recommend upgrading if you plan on doing this routine because it has been game changing. So every day you go in and it starts off with five deep breathes, then three to five minutes of a video that talks about things around you, such as the flow of water, etc. Then it gives you an option of three, five, ten minute meditations on the topic they pick that day, then the last piece of it is a program you pick—so each day you get to get a new meditation to help with the path you picked. So, for example, I have been dealing with a lot of pain, so I picked a pain management one. Each day it is something slightly different, but building on the day before; there are three levels and ten sessions in each. It also tracks your minutes you've done all together and your stroke of how many days in a row you have done. They also give you a midday workout if you want, and then to finish it up is a nighttime sleep support. I LOVE these nighttime stories.

Growing up, I had this old radio in my room (it was new then, but now they seem old because you don't see them anymore). I remember I would let it play while I was lying in bed and one night I stumbled upon a late night story. Someone would go on the radio and tell a story and I loved it! I think it came on at nine or ten at night, and I would love falling asleep to it. This sleep cast is very similar but they add in a meditation aspect, like deep breathing or visualization. I usually fall asleep within ten minutes or less and the cast is for forty-five minutes! Highly recommend this.

Once I have completed the four steps with my meditation app, I grab my *Unlimited by Zehra Mahoon* book. It is forty days of Law of Attraction work to help with manifestation. Every day has a new affirmation and a blurb about it. Then you say a little good morning passage—it is the same passage every morning, but I am not religious so I change Dear God to Dear Universe. I couldn't wrap my head around the God talk (which I am not against, just not my realm of belief—to each their own! No judgement on my end). I found this helped me get more into it.

Then it suggests self or guided meditation for fifteen to twenty minutes—which I now do before I start the book. Then it prompts you to write down five things you love and appreciate in your life, then three things that you hope to accomplish that day, then three things you would like the Universe to help you with. Next it gives you six things to bless—home, body, food, loved ones, work, and a blank one if you want to add others.

Then it gives you the same visualization to say every day about how good your life is. After that the last two are left for nighttime. It prompts you to write something about your day and then end with a good night Universe blurb similar to the morning one.

Once this piece is completed I will either pick up a book I am reading and read a chapter or a few pages of it, or I will write in my journal. It depends if I have something I need to get out on paper or not. If I don't have anything coming to mind I usually will read my book first, as a lot of times it prompts me to think of things. These books are usually some sort of growth or personal development, so most have something you can write about.

Journaling

If nothing comes to mind then I will save my journaling until the night or sometimes in the middle of the day. Sometimes I will write in it numerous times a day! Just really depends what is needed. I love writing and so this has been so enjoyable. I end the session with assessing my energy level out of ten and any sort of mood or symptoms I am having. It makes me really aware of what days I am feeling what and if something has triggered the moods or energy.

In the past I was always scared to put a pen to paper to write down how I am really feeling. It always felt like if I wrote it down, it was true. And usually I would write negative but try to positive spin it because I felt I was supposed to. Which really messed me up—thinking I couldn't be myself even to a book. That is not good. SO I have rekindled that relationship and things have been going really well and now it feels weird when I miss a day to write in it. Journaling is a great way to get everything out because it will just flow if you listen to yourself.

If you are like I was, and worried that people would read what I wrote or it made it real, I would recommend writing it out and then burning it or tossing it out at the bottom of the garbage. Getting things out can be so therapeutic. I highly recommend, even if you are scared. Just get it out of you, because bottling up and being the person you think others want you to be . . . is not a good way to live, and it can affect your immune system!

Movement

Once everything is done and I feel good, I will then start the rest of my day, which has some sort of movement in it—a walk, workout, or a dance party in my bathroom or kitchen. Moving your body is sooooo important for your mental health and physical body, as well how we deal with our stress and emotions. There are a lot of free options out there and honestly, stop making the excuses! Just do it. If you pick to go for a walk around the neighbourhood rather than plop down on the couch with a bag of chips and Netflix on the TV, I promise you that you will feel better then you did just sitting there. By all means sit and watch after—BUT get that body moving first. Not only will your mental health thank you but you will sleep better, have better mood regulating, and overall you will feel better about yourself.

Celebrate the Small Wins

Make sure you celebrate the little wins, though. Sometimes fitness can feel overwhelming, and when you celebrate when you do something, it helps you want to continue and do more. Celebrate putting your shoes on even if you don't go for that walk; you got one step closer than you did the day before. Be gentle with yourself on this journey but absolutely celebrate the damn wins! It doesn't just have to be about fitness, any little wins in your life, CELEBRATE them!

Viewing Our Bodies

Next, throughout the day I will catch myself in the mirror, and I will say something nice to myself. For the longest time I would avoid looking in the mirror because I didn't like who I was. I didn't like what I stood for, I didn't agree with my body; I actually hated it. Something shifted one day. I was walking by the mirror, and I stopped dead in my tracks and said, "Damnnnn girl you look good!" No clue where it came from but it put a huge smile on my face and I told myself that no matter what, I should always say something nice to myself when I look in the mirror. So far it has been working extremely well. I actually love my body and I am taking care of it more.

Water and Nutrition

I make sure to get as much water in me in the day as I can. Water is so, so important to the body and regulating everything. I find I am more likely to drink water than pop or anything else now. Before, you couldn't make me drink water. Now it is with me almost always. With this, I have been learning about food and how it affects my body; most foods my body hates. It would cause me so much pain, discomfort, bloating, gut issues, and major weight gain. I was putting everyone else first with what they liked, rather than what my body NEEDS. This was a huge shift for me because since changing that piece, I am not in pain every time I eat, I am not in the bathroom more times than not. My body is appreciating this way more.

Relationships

I realized that the people I surround myself with dictate how I am going to feel, act, the choices I make. If you are around people who like to eat junk food, drink heavy, don't exercise and are super nega-tive, do you think you are going to want to focus on any of your dreams or anything good for you? Probably not. I highly recommend looking at who is around you and who has influence on your mood and day. If you are finding no one in your group of friends is successful or doing things you want to do, you probably will lose all motivation. I can say I witnessed this firsthand. And since I have stepped back from some people, things are opening up to having met some AMAZING people who are more in line with what I am looking to do. It has been a huge shift with my relationships.

I have heard from many people that each person who comes into your life is for one of these three reasons:

1. They are in your life for a season
2. They are in your life for a reason
3. They are in your life for a lifetime

Now, a season can be any length of time; it is something that ultimately you decide. Try not to think about a season as winter, summer, fall, and spring. Although sometimes people only stay in your life for a couple months and that is okay! Anyone who comes into your life, try to figure out the why; that way you have an idea before committing time and effort into someone.

I have come across a lot of people. Sometimes I meet people just to meet someone in their circle to up my life—this would be a reason. I have people in my life who I am hanging on to for a season—right now I am in a growth season, this could last for months or years. And I have a select few who are in my life for a lifetime. One of them being my best friend. We have been friends for many, many years and we ended up getting tattoos together. I have on my leg: "She keeps me safe." She is like a mama bear to me! And she has on her leg: "She keeps me wild," because I am more the go getter to do fun things! Together we are amazingly hilarious, and I know she always has my back.

The people you surround yourself with are a reflection of you. If you had badass people who are upping their game or pushing you to up yours, you will succeed far more. If you hang out with people who don't share your values or desires, or heck, maybe you don't even want to tell them good news, they don't belong in your life. They are just bringing you down. And hey, if you are okay with that, that is fine! Everything in your life is your decision.

Your Mind is a Muscle

Okay, this one was a new one for me. I never thought about working your mind muscle. I always just listened to what people would tell me and I just believed them. I realized I was missing out on a lot of information because I would pick to put the TV on in the background rather than listen to something I can learn from.

I now do two things—I make sure every day I listen to a podcast or some sort of learning. Whether it is a Facebook Live that I came across on a topic I am interested in, or it is a podcast from one of my favourites. I have a few typical people I listen to that really amp me up.

Great example is that I have been toying with joining a Mastermind class, I have had numerous opportunities and I usually get excited and then I didn't follow through because of money. I kept putting money blocks up. Thinking about spending X amount of money made me nervous because what if I could not pay my bills then?

I have been wanting to join this specific Mastermind that I got a bit of a free version of from a challenge I joined, and because of this free version, I finally got the confidence to actually publish this book! The people I met in the group were amazing and in the same kind of boat I was. It was so nice to connect with likeminded people (again, my point above under relationships). So the coach told us about the full Mastermind class that was looking for founding members. I was like YES, I am IN! Next thing I know, I am pushing aside signing up because doubt crept in.

So yesterday I was looking for a podcast to listen to and it was about money and time. And literally in the episode it felt like they were talking to me, directly! And I will never forget a quote from it: *Education will make you money.* And the one takeaway they had was, "I wish I hired a coach sooner in life. Once I hired my coach, money flowed in. The knowledge and support I gained from that coaching was priceless and helped bring in a ton more money, more then I spent."

Wow. I had not even considered that spending money could actually make you more money. Mind you, I am not talking about buying that expensive workout gear, but specifically education. After listening to this episode I said out loud, "Okay, I am doing this! I am going to do this Mastermind and reap the benefits with a grateful heart." Podcasts have taught me WAY more than I ever would have learned by listening to the TV or Music.

Don't get me wrong, music is a huge part of my life and a big mood lifter but I don't learn anything from it, and in a season of learning and growing, I need to have a balance.

Speaking of balance, on top of the podcasts, I read, every day. Now sometimes I will read self-help books, or some sort of learning books where it gets me thinking or working on something in my journal. I use these kinds of books for my morning routine and I just read a chapter or more if I want or have time. I also make sure to make a point to read fiction books. I LOVE reading, and mystery/thriller books are my favourite because I can "escape" life by imagining the story playing out. It is much different than watching a movie, because reading a book you actually get to make up how the character looks. You get some idea from the book, but ultimately they will appear in your mind.

Sometimes I can read half a book in a couple hours and if I really enjoy it I find I turn the TV on way less, and I actually stop and read. This is part of my self care as well. I love reading, and it calms me. I always feel good after I read.

So my tip to you is to try to figure out how you can learn or grow and implement this into your life any time you can. I promise you that you will always learn something and you will continue to grow! Get reading and listening to learning!

Social Media

Post the damn picture. Don't be so worried that people are going to pick you apart. In the world of social media, there will always be haters and trolls. Just ignore them or block them. Take NOTHING they say to heart because they don't know you. They are hiding behind a screen where nothing can hurt them and they can say whatever they want. They don't care. They hate their lives so they make others feel bad to make themselves feel better.

I also highly recommend taking social media detoxes; stay off there for a couple of days. It will be a game changer to realize how other people don't have to affect your life; you will go on if they are there or not. Just try it. I promise you will be okay to not be checking notifications every moment. It also shows you how addicted you are to your phone!

Gratitude/Positive Moments

I try to end the day thinking about all the good things that happened, to end on a good note. If we constantly think about the bad, that is what we will consume ourselves with. If you can distract yourself from the negative by throwing positive in its face then you are laughing! It changes your mood instantly. I also find if you can't think of anything positive or that you are grateful for, then send a note or call a friend, and tell them what you are grateful for them. Maybe you are just grateful they have your back, or let you vent, or maybe they are pushing you to do better. Tell them. I guarantee that they will love it, and you may even make their day better!

The last piece of my day ends with filling in the last part of my *Unlimited by Zehra Mahoon* book. It asks you to put something down about your day, and then there is a little bedtime mantra. I just love this; it has really helped me stay focused, and I feel the changes flowing!

Ultimately it is up to you ...

What you have just read is a lot of the things I am focusing on but it has to work for you. The worst is when someone tells you to do something and you just can't get into it, so then you dread doing it. That is NOT what this is for. You need to do things that make you happy and fill you up. Only do a morning routine if you know what your purpose is. If you don't know why you are doing it, or you are doing things that don't make sense for what you are looking for, then don't do it. Figure out the why and you will be able to stick to it. If you just jump in and don't know the why, then you will quit and I don't want you to miss out on a life you love.

My best advice would be to try different things, but give them time to work out. I almost gave up on my meditation, and it took about two weeks of doing it consistently to find that if I don't do it, I have a hard time with the day—my mood is not as good as it could be. Just give it time and a try, what do you have to lose?

My journey is just starting and taking form. I have no idea what is in store in the future but things are looking brighter and more likely for the best life possible. All I had to do was try to be consistent. I did it for myself and myself alone. No one forced me. Do something for you.

I have found a really awesome habit tracker called Habitica. It is free and you get to create your own character and get pets! Might sound weird but you can track habits or a To Do list in there. It is a great space to keep track of things.

Vibrations

Have you ever been a part of something, or met someone that just amped you up? Like, gave you chills and pumped you right up? This, my dear, is what is called vibrations. Everyone has them. But some people are very low and some are very high. You know the people who just seem to get everything they ask for or just are really happy people? That is someone who is on a high vibration or frequency. Someone who is negative and constantly saying they hate their life or their job etc., they are on the very low end of the spectrum.

Want to know the trick to the happiness vibration? They believe they already have the thing they want, or outcome they want. They believe they already have it and they put it out in the universe. Not like praying for it, but just saying, "I have five thousand dollars in my account right now." Keep saying it and it can appear. It sounds simple but it is actually not as easy as one would think. You have to fully believe it and you need to fully be invested in the process. This means letting go of your shit. Letting go of the past, the pain, the what ifs, the negative talk. If all that still stems from you, then you will never get to be at the top of the vibrations.

I will tell you, I am not there yet. But I am working on it. Learning different things to do is also very helpful—such as moon rituals, clearing your space of negative energy by smudging, journaling, talking to a counselor, etc. One of the biggest things I have learned lately is that you cannot pour from an empty cup. Find what lights you up, and make sure you do that every day. You are worth happiness!

Fuck Cancer

I always knew cancer was a bad thing. You just hear the word and you want to spit on it. I didn't think cancer would ever be in my family. Just felt like it was out of reach to get us. Unfortunately, my mom was diagnosed with Non-Hodgkin's Lymphoma. Basically, my mom's body was riddled with cancer in her lymph nodes. The messed up part? She wasn't really sick to the point that signs would be showing up to be tested for cancer. She also has fibromyalgia so she gets tired and sore but this was something different. I remember back to a day when I was struggling with my health, and my mom had an appointment for a physical booked and she offered

it to me (we have the same doctor). I said, "No, it's okay, you keep
the appointment."

During that appointment, my mom's entire life changed. The
doctor was pressing on my mom's stomach and it was painful. She
was concerned enough to send my mom for blood work and some
tests. At first I had no idea this was happening. My mom and dad
hid it VERY well. To the point where we were going to Hawaii for
Christmas and they were not showing that they had any issues; we
had no idea something was wrong. I was actually flying out from
Hawaii to meet my friend in Vancouver to fly out to Thailand for
two months. The month of January I wasn't in touch too much with
my parents, other than letting them know I was alive.

Our trip ended early and I got back home at the end of January.
That following week was one of the worst ones I have had with my
family. I remember coming home from a friends house and walking
into the house; my smile dropped. Something was wrong. My mom
and sister were in tears, sitting down with my dad who had a very
worried look on his face. I instantly felt sick. *What is happening?*

We were told that my mom might have cancer and we were
waiting on some tests. I remember going with her to the hospital
for a colonoscopy to see if the cancer was in her stomach, or in that
general area. She came out with a diagnosis of no cancer. We were
all so excited that night we had a little dance party. The next day,
my mom got a call from the doctor saying that there was no cancer
in her stomach or bowel, but that didn't rule it out somewhere else.

We instantly broke down. How can they say no cancer on the
form and then get told, "Well, they meant no cancer in this area . . ."
That was an awful way to put it. *BE MORE SPECIFIC*, I remember
yelling inside. How can they do this to people? How can they make
you feel such a relief to then ruin it again?

She had to do a different test, a scan of some sort. That confirmed
it. There were lumps in her body. They did a biopsy of a lump in her
neck and we got the news: Non-Hodgkin's Lymphoma, not curable,

nonaggressive, but treatable. So basically she would never be rid of it, but needed to get it in remission.

I remember vividly the night we got the confirmed cancer diagnosis. I was so upset in my room. I decided to call my boyfriend at the time to come over. I didn't tell him why, I just said I needed him. He came over in his goofy mood and I was not having it. In between sobs I told him my mom had cancer. I thought for sure he would understand since his dad had cancer and had died from it.

But instead, he said to me, "I had a really bad day too. I realized the insurance on my car is expiring two days before I get paid and I might not be able to renew right away."

I was speechless. I stared at him and held my breath.

The next thing I knew, I was telling him to go and that I wouldn't be able to see him much for a bit as I needed to be with my family. Clearly he didn't understand. He would call me and get upset I wasn't spending time with him or giving him attention. One night he got drunk and told me I wasn't being fair to him, saying that I should be there for him.

I ended the relationship shortly afterwards. He continued to pursue me, showing up at my work, my house, and anytime he saw me driving around he would follow me. Just to talk to me.

A few months later I decided life was short and I needed to move; I ended up moving to Alberta, and he showed up on one of my last days at work, to beg me to stay and marry him. Needless to say, I didn't.

My mom went through chemo for six months and had a hell of a time recovering. By the way, chemo brain is a thing. The amount of things my mom forgot was crazy! I know it was making life difficult for her. Slowly things got better.

Around the point where it would have been about five years in remission, my mom had some issues with her throat. She didn't have much of a voice, her throat hurt and she found a lump on the side of her neck. She went in for a check up with her doctor.

It was the first week of February, the day before my parents were supposed to be flying out to Hawaii for some time together after a tough year and to celebrate my dad's birthday. They received a call from my mom's doctor. Cancer was back, but different. This time it was aggressive and curable. Which was good and bad. Good because it was curable, bad because it was aggressive. So not only did they have to cancel their trip and try to get money back, but they had to go through this all again. I remember this one was a lot harder on her, we had to get on chemo right away. The hospital got her in for chemo five days later, on my dad's birthday. I went with them so my dad didn't have to do it alone. It was a full day at the hospital and then back again the next day.

Because of the chemo treatment the last time, my mom's veins were just not holding up well. The nurses had a very difficult time finding the vein for the IV. In the end she had to get a PICC line put in, which is basically an IV that stays in your arm that goes up to your heart so that the chemo gets into the blood stream. Whenever I was around my mom I felt like I was going to hurt her with the PICC sticking out. But she was so strong. One of the strongest women I know.

I can't speak to how it is having cancer, but I can share my experience of what it was like to have someone I care about going through cancer, and not just one time. If you are going through this, please seek help from a counselor or therapist. Or if that isn't an option, try to find support groups. Being able to talk about how you feel with others is so helpful. I remember I tried to be so strong for my family, I tried to not cry or be sad around them. I hid it pretty well I think. I was lucky to have some friends who had gone through it with a loved one. The first bit is really hard because you literally feel numb trying to process it.

Just know that they need you and they are trying to be strong for you. My mom is a warrior and I am so proud of her for kicking ass again. I really hope that the cancer doesn't come back, but if it does, I have faith she will beat it again!

FUCK CANCER!

"The best feeling in the whole world is watching things finally fall into place after watching them fall apart for so long."

—LiveLifeHappy.com

CHAPTER 10

WORDS FROM MY PAST

Dear Me,
You've been through a lot. I know it's hard but I'm so proud of
who you are. You are strong, brave, bright, and smart, and you
were given the gift of a beautiful heart. So keep going strong and
try not to stray. Everything you're praying for is on its way.
Love,
Me

When I was younger I loved to write in my journal, write poems, and write stories. It was my way of getting things out, as I used to bottle up everything inside of me. I remember when I was a teenager we had these big fat computers that took up half of the desk it was on because the back of it was so long. We had the computer set up in my dad's office, and I would have my time on the computer where I would talk to my friends. I would also go on and type out the stories that I wrote, and save them on a floppy disk. I would save my stories on it and hope that I didn't break it. I still to this day found my printed copies of these stories and I still have the books where I wrote my poems in.

Some of the things I wrote about at the same age as my step-daughter is what she is going through as well. It is interesting to see how she feels about boys compared to how I did. If a breakup occurred, it was the end of the world. Same for her.

I hope my words will help someone in a time of need, or just make them feel less alone. I never really named my poems, so they are unnamed in this book.

Walking down a street, as if there is nowhere left to go
Tears descend down her soft cheeks
A path they were known to take.
Tripping over her own tears, crashing to her knees.
Another piece of her broken heart crumbles to the ground
The rain cascades down, on this late autumn evening
Dark clouds, no blue sky in sight, just the way she feels.
Her tears increase, body shivering as the temperature drops
No sign of hope or faith could be found within her
All the pain and suffering fills her mind, heart and soul.
She always let her wall down too fast, made too many mistakes
The one thing she wanted more than ever was to be loved
As she still knelt in her now puddle of rain and tears.
All she could do was blame herself

+ 2 +

From the depth of my soul
To the tears in my eyes
My screams of pain echo
Alone and unhappy once again
Smiles and laughter disappear
Feeling of safety and warmth gone
The one true thing I thought I had
Feelings from the unknown
Come crashing down in the wink of an eye
Pieces of my heart crumble down
Tears descend down my cheeks
As I crouch in the corner
Wondering why always the wrong, next to the right
Never good enough for anything, anyone
Never to be cared about, loved
Body trembling and shaking
Swollen eyes, wet cheeks
Loss of hope and faith

+ 3 +

Through the depths of despair I face
The coldness steals my breath away
The wind pulls my body
Freeing the tears in my swollen eyes
Down, down, down that is all that I know
Reaching for the future but stuck in the past
Heartache and blame is all that I contain
Surrounded by emptiness
Captured by pain
Unwillingness to free myself and start over again
Light disappears
Cascading a cloud of darkness to fulfill the spot
Body shaking
Eyes burning
Heart crumbling
This is all that I know
Forever and Always

+ 4 +

Having you near me
I've never felt more far away
I urge to feel close to you again
Before it's too late
The tears that stream down
Burn like fire
My dreams filled with heartache
Night after night
Missing the love and laughter
The gap between us is growing
Love is fading
Dreams and the future are fading
I've never loved anyone as much as I do you
That's why this hurts so badly
Losing you would mean losing a part of myself
I want you to be my knight
My saviour and my soulmate
I can't fight or hurt anymore
I am not sure what more there is to say
Other than I miss how we used to be

+ 5 +

The world rains down with the bad
Emotions flying around
Feelings lingering in the air

Yelling at the darkness
Getting frustrations out
Tears streaming down

Love and tenderness disappear
Emptiness, all alone
Strangled by the deafening sound of silence

+ 6 +

Lost in the mist
Broken in the unknown world
Never fitting in
Always feeling dull or alone

Just wanting to be accepted
Searching to find myself
Happiness has fallen down a waterfall of tears
Laughter hiding in the shadows

Love seems to be meaningless
Promises always broken
Dreams shattered
Forgiveness lost
Memories faded

+ 7 +

When someone you love passes
Your love does not fade
The sadness and tears linger for awhile
But the pain they suffered from disappears.

God took him from us
Not to punish
But to relieve the pain and suffering
Taking him to a pain free and happy place.

The sadness and tears will vanish
But memories will last forever
His smile would light up the room
His laughter warmed your heart
He tried to make it to all family get-togethers
He never forgot holidays or birthdays.

Never forget the ones you love
They are watching over you
Hoping you are safe and happy.

Make sure you live your life to the fullest
Telling the ones close to you "I love you"
Never forgetting those you made you who you are
Be strong and love life
He would have wanted it that way.

+8+

Golden beams of sun
Touch the blue tips of the sea
Her feet wiggle in the sand
Looking up at the magnificent view
Makes her wonder…why?
She was all alone on a beach
Which felt so far away from anyone
Her eyes teared up
A breeze pushed her hair off her shoulder
A shiver shook through her body
The waves of the beautiful sea touched her toes
She looked out over the horizon
Slowly closed her eyes
Felt as if someone was right beside her
The breeze came again
Only this time she heard a whisper
    "Don't stop looking, your one step closer.
    Don't stop searching, it's not over.
    Don't let go, love will find you"
She opened her eyes with a new outlook
A new hope in her heart
The strength she needed to survive

+9+

Floating in a sea of tangerine bubbles
Sipping on chamomile apple tea
Soft music in the background
    "Hanging on to every word you say…"
Waiting for the year to come to an end
Thinking about the need for validation
The past is the past
The bad things make you stronger
Give you strength and understanding
Or so they say
What if you hurt too much?
Can't sleep due to nightmares?
Can't feel or trust anyone?
Willing to do anything to feel wanted
When really it makes the lonely pain stick around
Validation in all the wrong ways
Maybe one day the pain will go away

+10+

Decisions, decisions, decisions
Falling down fast
Money dwindling
Mind fluttering, unsure, scared
Living in a place I hate
But surrounded by loving family
Move to a place unknown
Having friendship to follow
New places, new beginnings
No expectations
Life in the mist
Finding myself, all on my own
Outta sight, outta mind
I believe...

+11+

Sittin', wishin', waitin'
Dodging the obstacles of the world
Battling to survive
Some barriers cannot be moved
Support is missing
Aggravation growing inside
Unhappiness filling the void
Past resentments linger, never to fade
Missed opportunities grow
Need to find a way to happiness
Get up and go
Fly with the broken wings
Keep the faith, you can survive

+12+

Happiness is within
Or so people keep saying
Every now and again I believe this
But then time and time again
I step outside my box
And overlook my world
I see that everyone is truly happy
Moving towards their futures with their family
I am missing so much in my life
My happiness is fake
Everyone tells me to be happy
But knocks down any of my ideas or dreams
How can I be happy or find myself
If the world is against me?
Happiness within is fake

+13+

Sometimes the world throws a lot of you
You think you can't handle it
And you break
Into a million pieces
The wind swoops them up
Scattering them all over
Fight the urge to give up
Learn from what happened
Pick up some of the pieces
Start to build new pieces
Fill the holes
Becoming a better version of you
Stronger, well rounded person
Who can love themselves
For who they are and not what was said
Believe in you

"You'll never break free from it, if you never take ownership of it."

–Trent Shelton

CHAPTER 11

UNAPOLOGETIC

Tell the story of the mountains you climbed. Your words could become a page in someone else's survival guide.

—Morgan Harper Nichols

Wow! You made it! You got through all of the stories, information, and support. I want to thank you for getting to this end chapter. I poured my heart and soul into this book in the hopes that someone will read it and it will help them. Not everyone is going to be able to get through this, as there are a lot of tough topics in here that can cause for some triggers, especially at the beginning. Which just means they have some demons to heal through too! We all have them. It is up to us to figure out how to get past them. Ain't nobody going to do it for us!

I think it is important to remember that your voice makes a difference. If you keep things bottled up or you don't fight for what you believe in, then you could be missing out on something better. Life can throw you crazy things to deal with, but the way I see it, if everything went smoothly in life it would be boring! So, yes, the hard times suck and the bad days can last longer then you want, but ultimately, it is up to you to change that.

The last year has been a whirlwind of learning and growing and finding out what my actual desires and dreams are. I got selfish. When I say that, I mean that I focused on me for once and took the time to do so. I was listening to one of Trent Shelton's podcast episodes recently, and he was talking about how we need to have more fun in life. That regardless of our age, we can be young in spirit. There are ninety-year-olds who do more things than most teens these days!

When we don't do things that bring us joy or protect our peace, we become boring. It is sad to think about—BUT if you think that your age does not define you, that you can be ninety-six and be more of a kid than a teenager is, you will get to do so many more things in life and you will not be bored. I don't want to be boring, and I certainly do not want to be on my death bed, regretting the things I did not do. Regretting not having more fun and stressing all the time.

Did you know that laughter is one of the best medicines for you? By medicine I don't mean it comes from a doctor, but it is something that is so good for your body. Laughter can take you out of a bad mood, laughter can make your abs hurt and your eyes cry. Laughter can bring you closer with people or closer with your inner self. Sometimes when I am feeling sad, I think to myself, *When was the last time I laughed? Like really, belly hurts from laughing, laughed?*

Sadly I have had to answer that lately, more often than not, I can't remember. COVID has really made things harder for people to connect, for people to feel free, for people to get out and do what they enjoy. Instead, we are stuck at home, feeling all the feels or maybe drinking them down. It has not been a positive place for many people, myself included.

With saying that though, it has given me more time to focus on myself. I have been able to really understand what I enjoy, what fills up my cup, what hurts me food-wise and what helps me get past my anxiety. There are so many tools out there, you just have to be willing to try them. I know I have tried many things and some stuck, and some did not. Either way, we are all different so what I find helpful, you may not. You just have to decide to be fully into figuring it out.

There are some things that I have done in the last year that have helped the process, and I wanted to share some of them with you to hopefully round this all out for you.

Learning style

One of the biggest things I have learned through this process is the best way that I learn and retain information. The ways that excite me to learn more and keep doing it out of habit. The way that I learn best or get motivated is through podcasts. I love listening to them and getting excited, inspired, motivated, thought processing or even just in the mood to groove. I also have a love for reading, but I find reading just gets me thinking rather than the other feelings above.

My suggestion to you would be to spend the time trying out different media platforms to see what best suits you for what you are trying to achieve. After you have used one, ask yourself, *How did that make me feel?* If you answer any of the feelings you wanted then you know that is an option of how you enjoy learning.

Remember, this is not a sprint; it is a long distance run. It is going to take time to grow and see changes. Soak in as much knowledge about yourself and grow as much as you can, every damn day.

Dreaming

Once you figure out the best way that you learn, your next job is to start dreaming. Dream big. Understand the world is your oyster!

The best way that I found to dream big was to build a bucket list! I highly recommend doing this, it creates excitement about things that you want to accomplish in life. It also starts to be a road map to what you may want to use on a goal board. I highly recommend if you are doing these two boards that you get bright poster board and things you can use on it to jazz it up! I have many colors and sparkles on mine.

Both boards can be whatever you want them to be. I would not set too many requirements for yourself. Pick what you want to see and know about yourself on it. Make it about you and no one else.

Once I got mine done, I hung them in my office so I look at them every day I am in there. It is a great reminder of what I want to accomplish in the year or in my life and what to focus on.

Dream big, my darling.

Mantra

I never really believed in this. Saying something to myself over and over again just seemed silly. But then I tried it . . . and it actually works. Not only does it help me with anxiety, but it also helps with keeping me calm, levelheaded, and confident. When I started working with mantras I would forget what it was supposed to be a bunch of times, until I found the book *Badass Habits* by Jen Sincero. It teaches you all about habits and then gives you twenty-one days of how to create a habit, and by the time I was done, my mantra was stuck in my head even when I had stopped thinking about it! I found myself repeating it without having to be reminded. It is a pretty cool feeling. I really resonated with this quote from *Badass Habits* by Jen Sincero: "You will experience whatever you believe. And you will believe whatever you repeatedly tell yourself is true." If we believe we are in a bad situation, then it will be a bad situation, and vice versa. Our minds believe what we tell them!

I highly recommend getting this book if you want to create new habits and work on mantras. Also if you pair that with the app called Habitica – which helps you track your habits and I spoke about it in another chapter- I am certain you will be doing awesome with habits and mantras!

Journaling

I have discussed this in a previous chapter, and how it has really helped me, but I found that when I started out I would not consistently journal every day. Not until I started working on habits and making sure I wrote it in every day regardless. It does not have to be pages every time you write, but just a simple couple of sentences is all you may need that day.

I find starting my day with this is amazing. It really sets the tone for me. Some days I like to write in it from prompts I get from all over the place—a book I am reading, a challenge I am doing online, or just looking them up online. I find having prompts helps you dig a bit deeper than just every day things that go wrong or the stress in your life. It also can help to see what you want your future to be like if you have not figured that out already.

I really like starting my day with, *I love and appreciate* . . . then I name five things under it. Some people do things they are grateful for which is similar. Then I write down three things that would be nice to have done that day and then I write down three things that I would like the universe to help me with that day.

You can get many prompts that talk about the past, the present, and the future; it all really depends on what you are looking to work on. I recommend trying out different kinds of prompts and different places to find them; as I said, I have them from all over and they offer different things, so it is helpful! Pinterest is a great resource to search for journal prompts.

Thank you

Truly, sincerely, thank you for taking the time to purchase and read my book. I hope that it has provided you with what you were looking for, or perhaps you found out something that surprised you or made you think.

If you think that this book can help someone out, please share it or tell them to go buy it! Sharing is caring after all! If you feel like it, please share a photo on your social media and tag me in it on Instagram @authornataliefrost—share what you learned, as I would love to hear from you. If you don't want to share on social media but you want to ask questions, please don't hesitate to contact me.

Thank you again and I am wishing you the best self-journey and I hope you come out the other side a better version of yourself. I am so proud of you, beautiful.

"Never be afraid to be yourself. It's one of the most powerful gifts you have. Change the world, don't let the world change you. Stay authentic."

—Trent Shelton

END NOTE

Ananias Foundation. n.d. "Abuse Definitions." Accessed August 20, 2021.
https://www.ananiasfoundation.org/definitions/

Government of Canada. 2018. "Family violence: How big is the problem in Canada?" Stop Family Violence. Last modified May, 31, 2018. Accessed August 20, 2021
https://www.canada.ca/en/public-health/services/health-promotion/stop-family-violence/problem-canada.html

Mayo Clinic. n.d. "Self-injury/cutting" Diseases & Conditions. Accessed August 20, 2021.
Self-injury/cutting - Symptoms and causes - Mayo Clinic

Wikipedia. n.d. "Ghosting" Last modified July 29, 2021, Accessed August 20, 2021
https://en.wikipedia.org/wiki/Ghosting